Butterfly Coloring Book for Adults

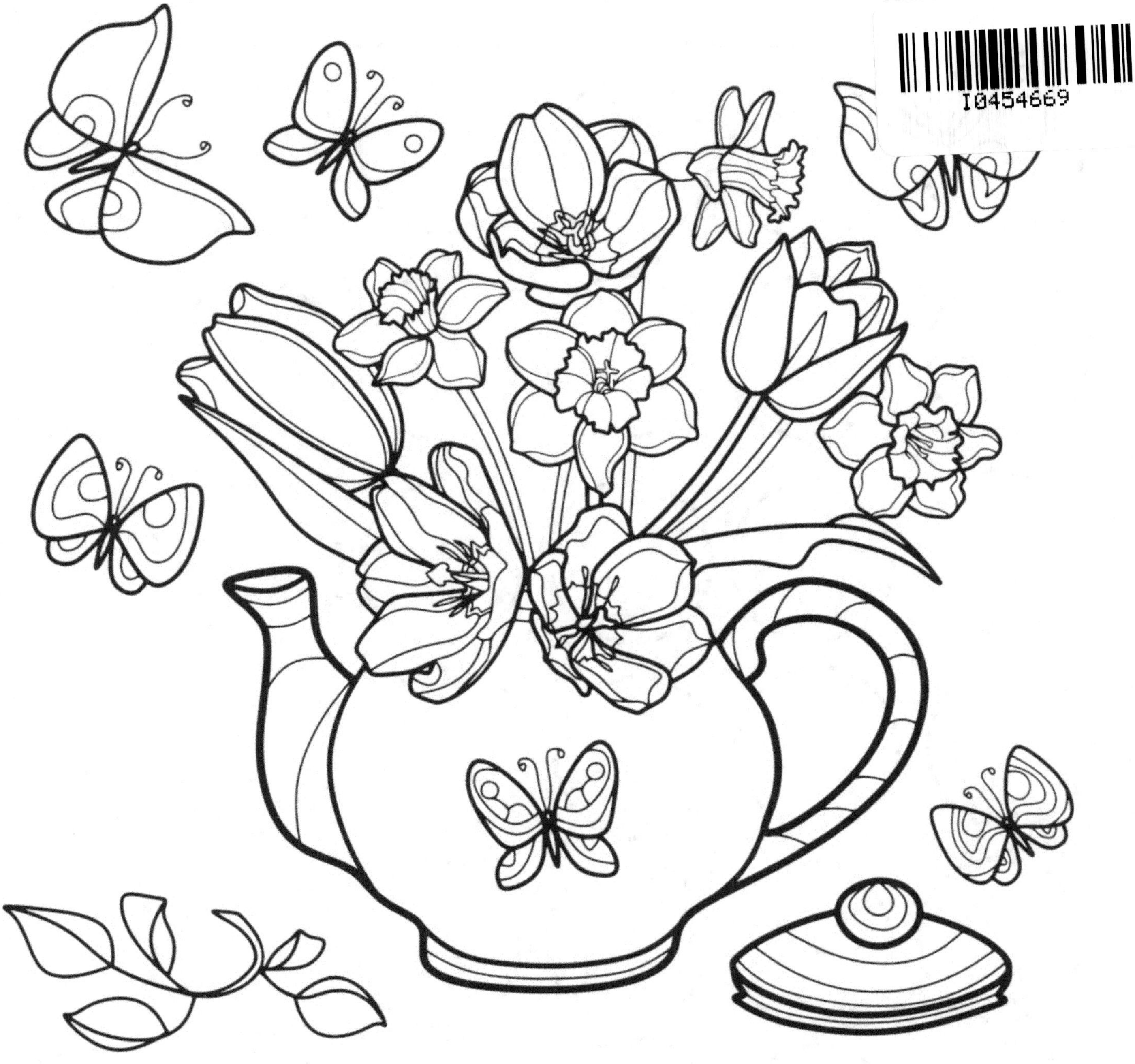

THIS BOOK BELONGS TO

....

....

COLOR TEST PAGES

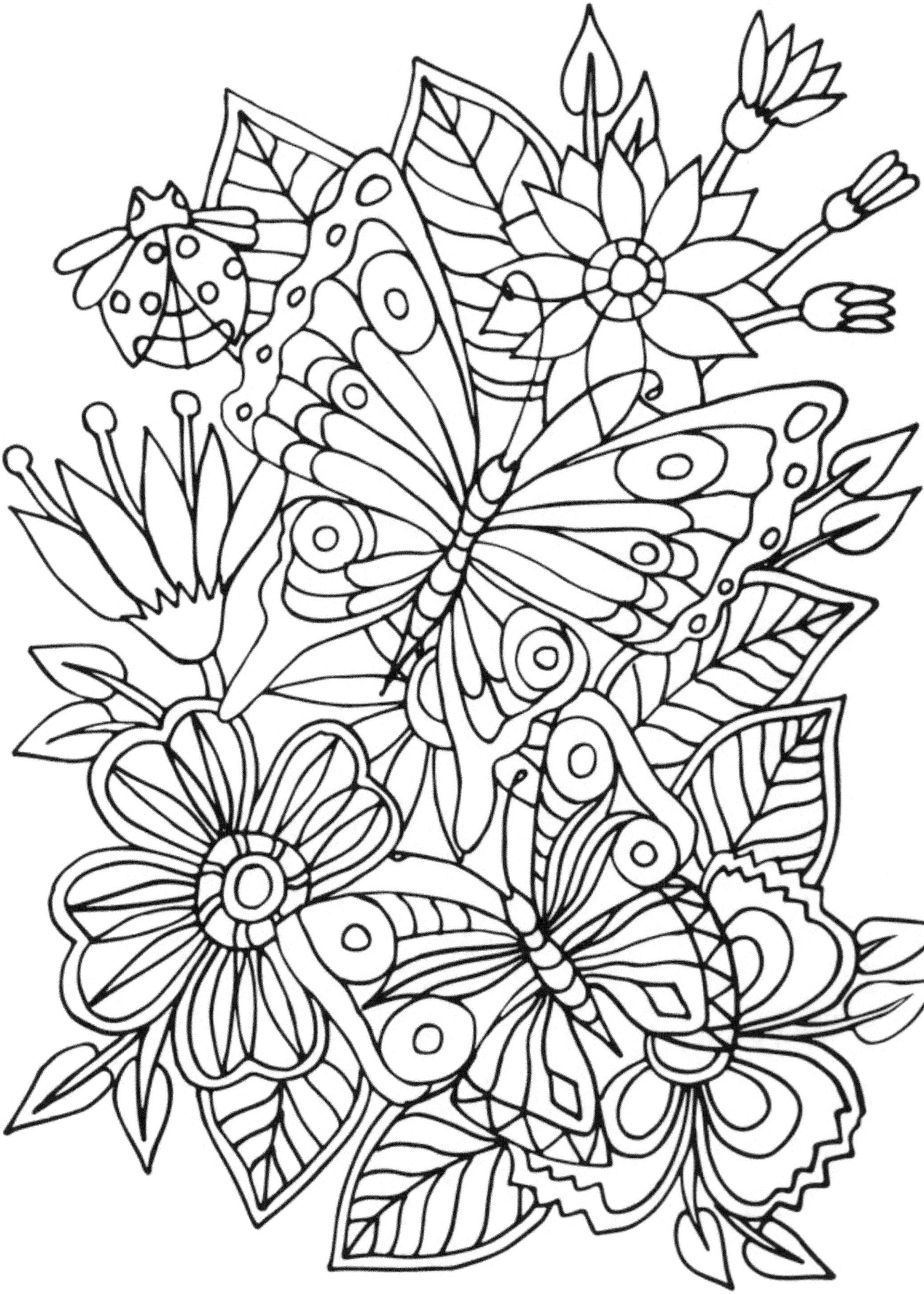

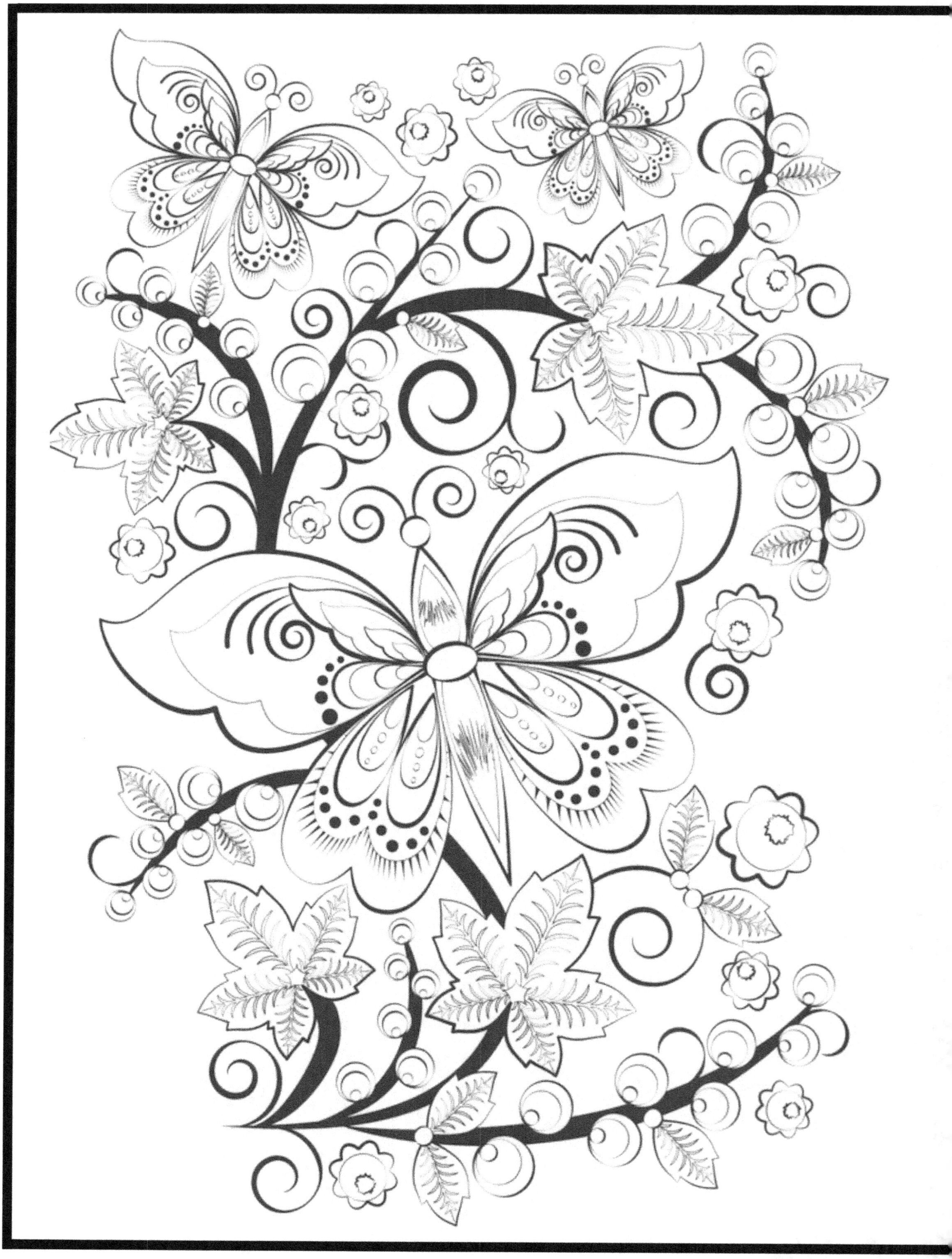

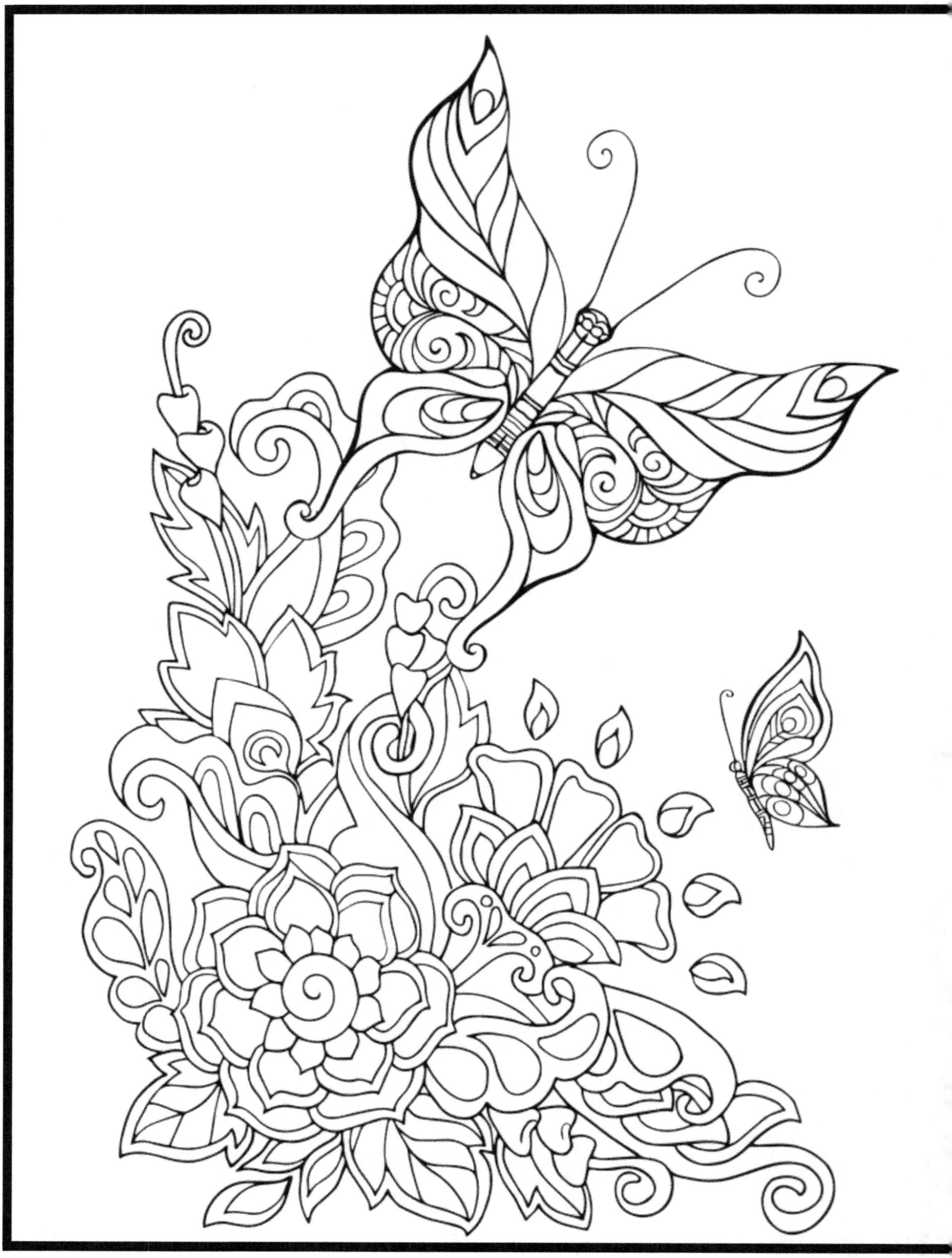

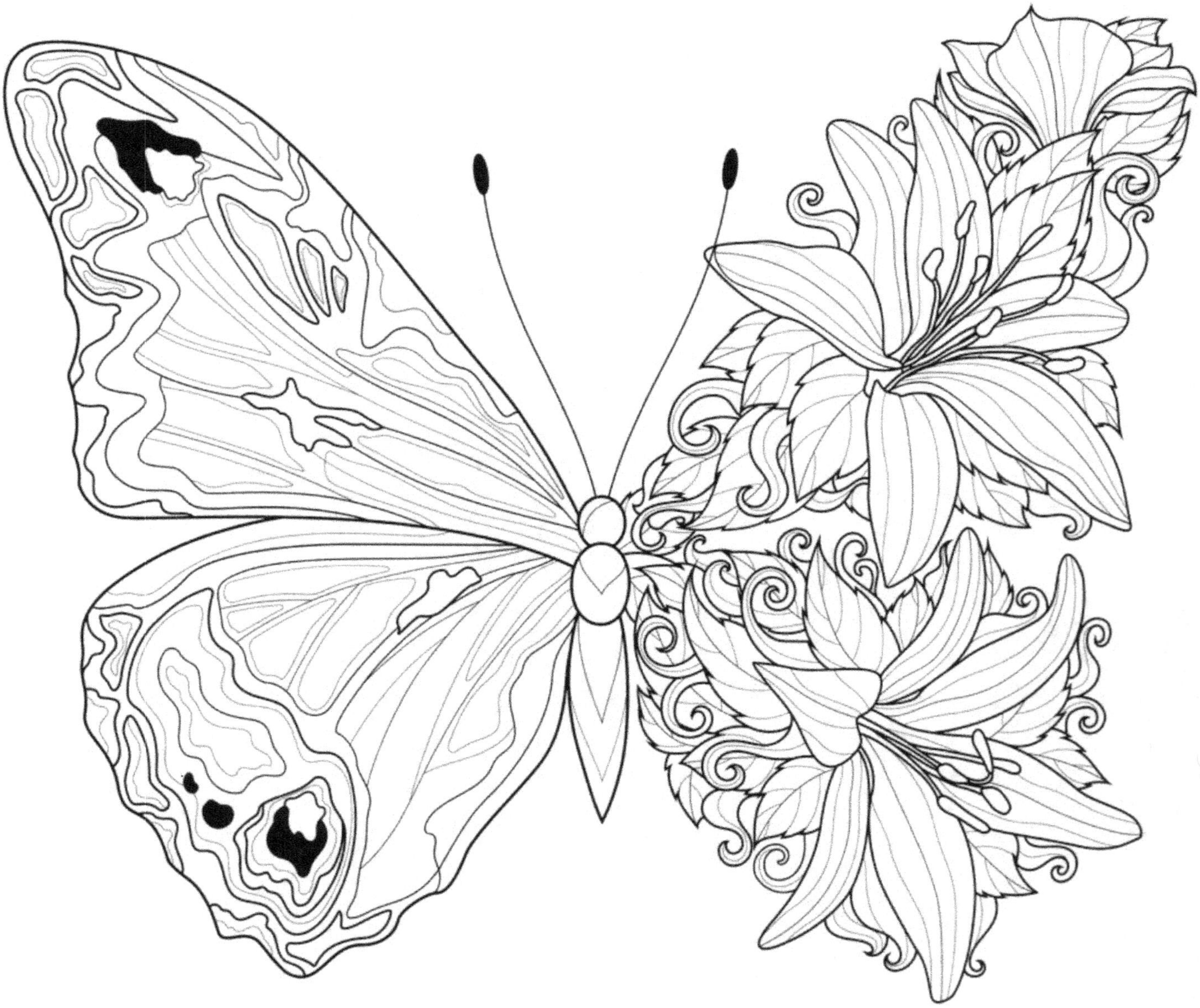

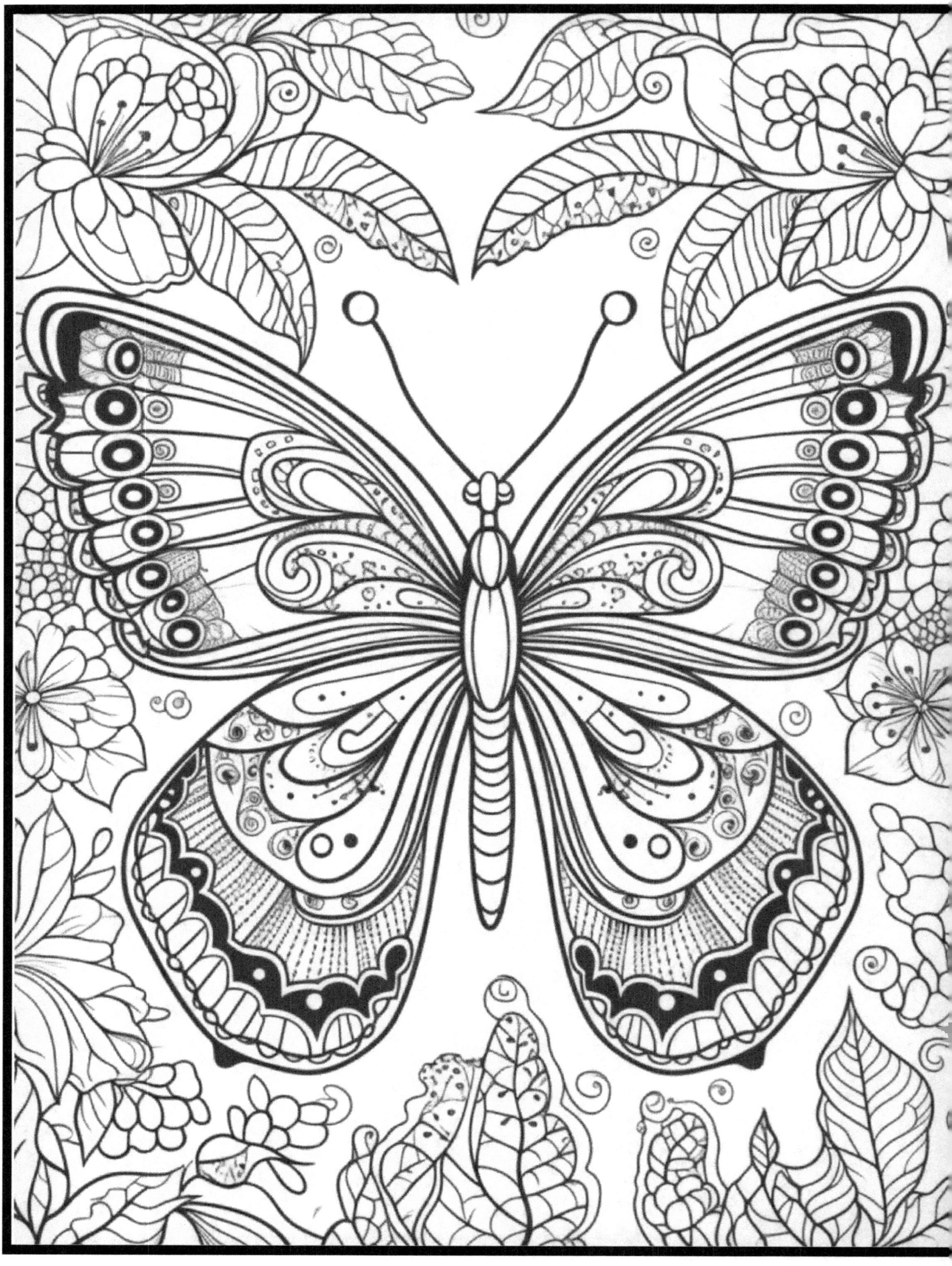

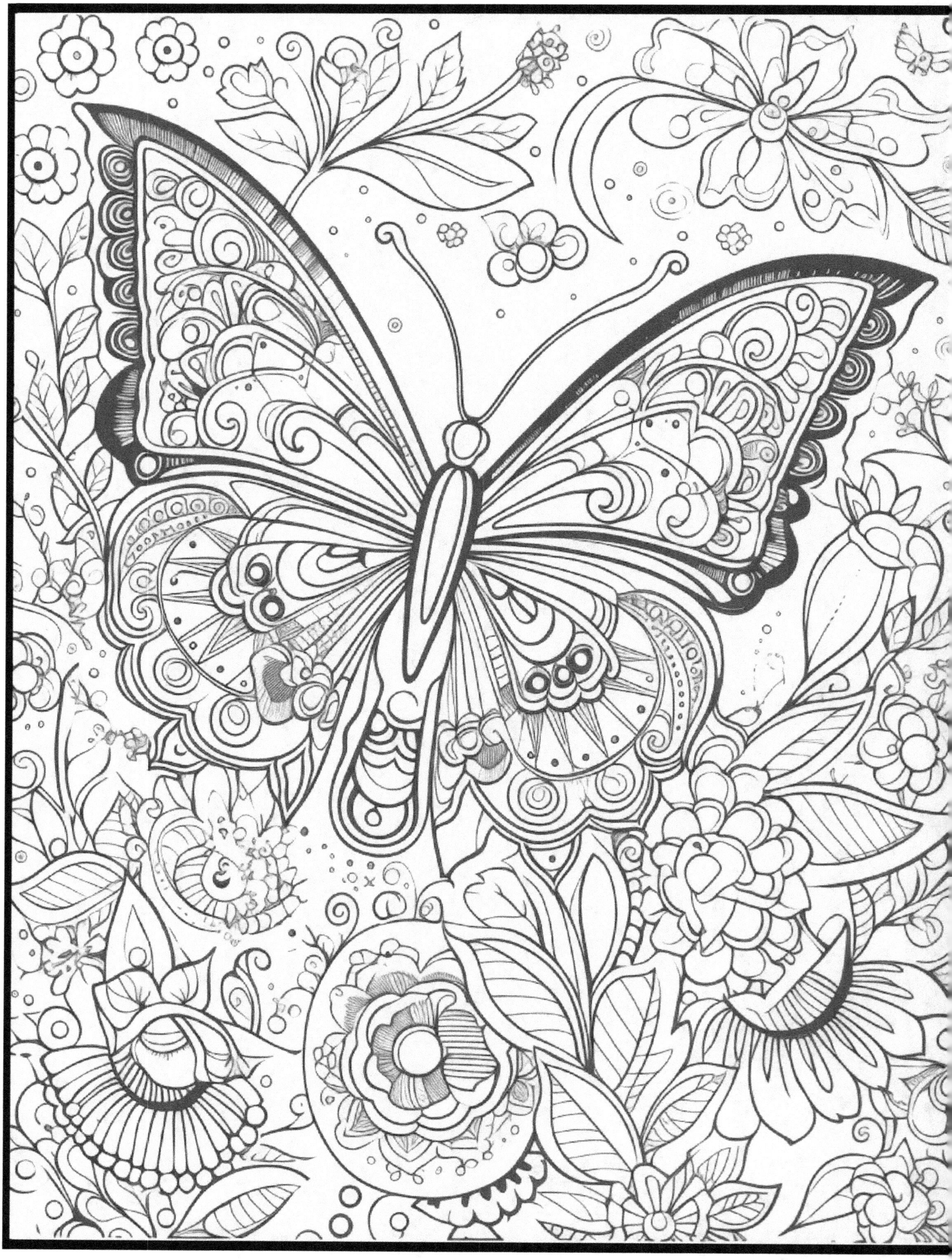

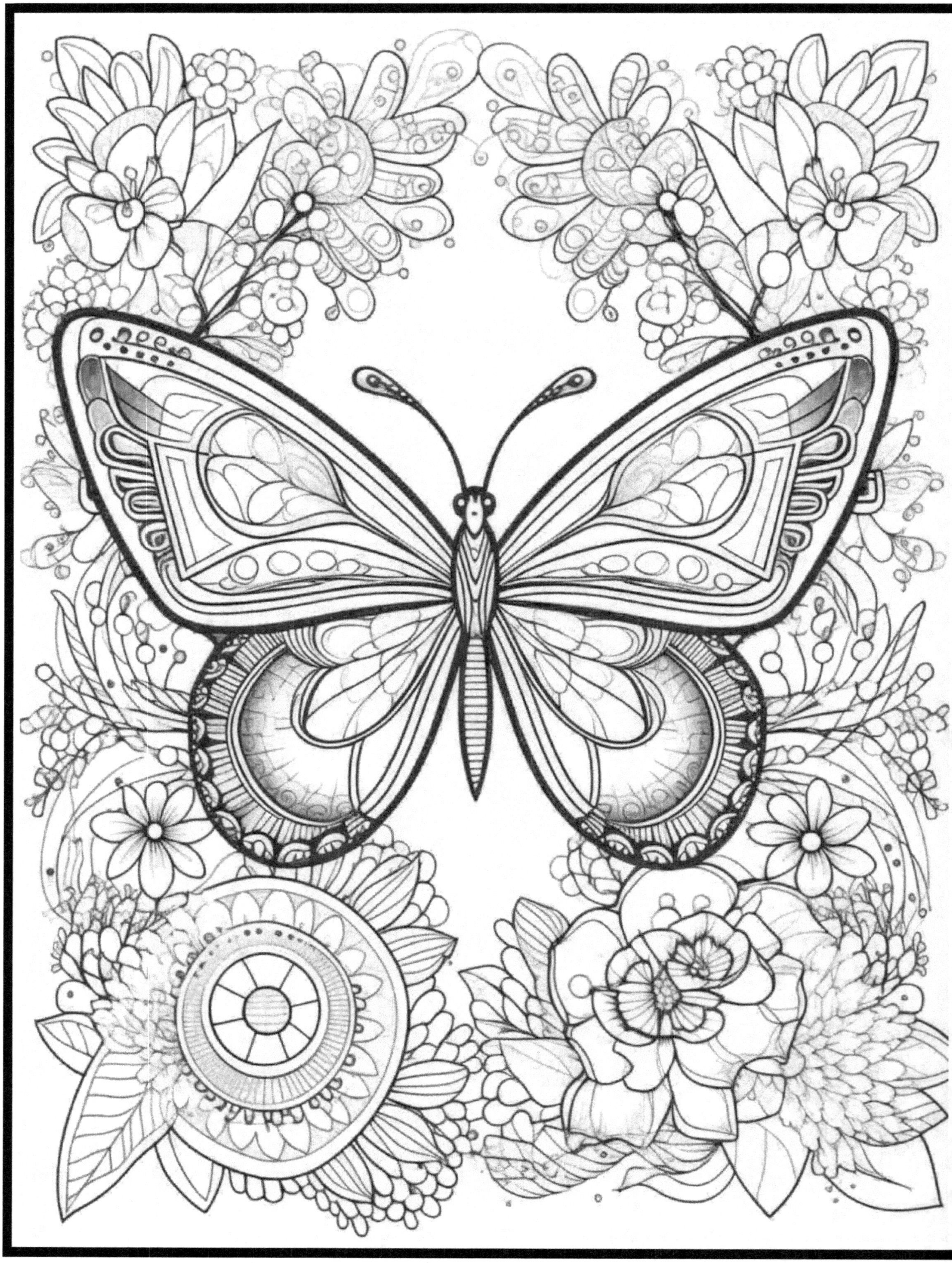

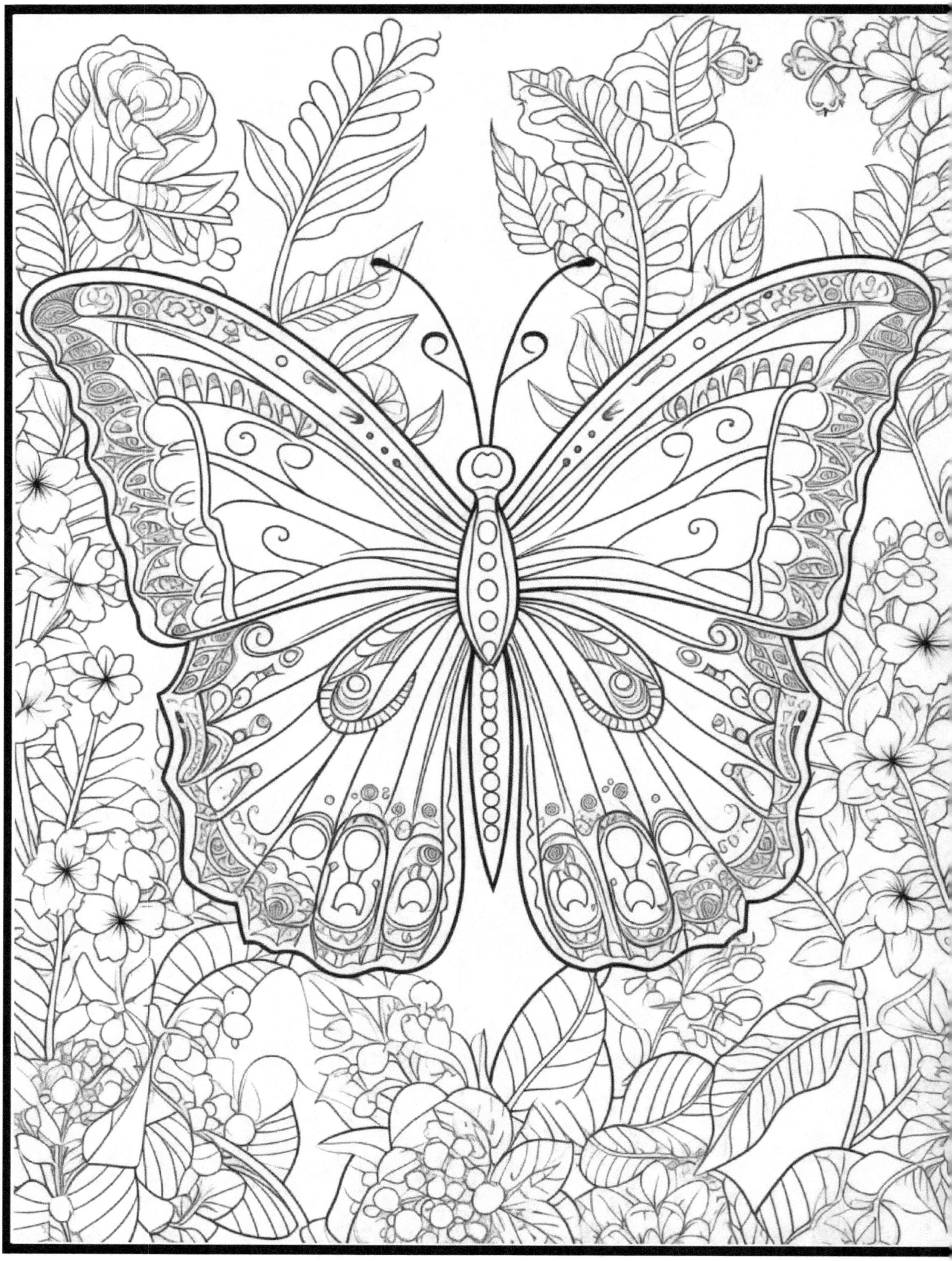

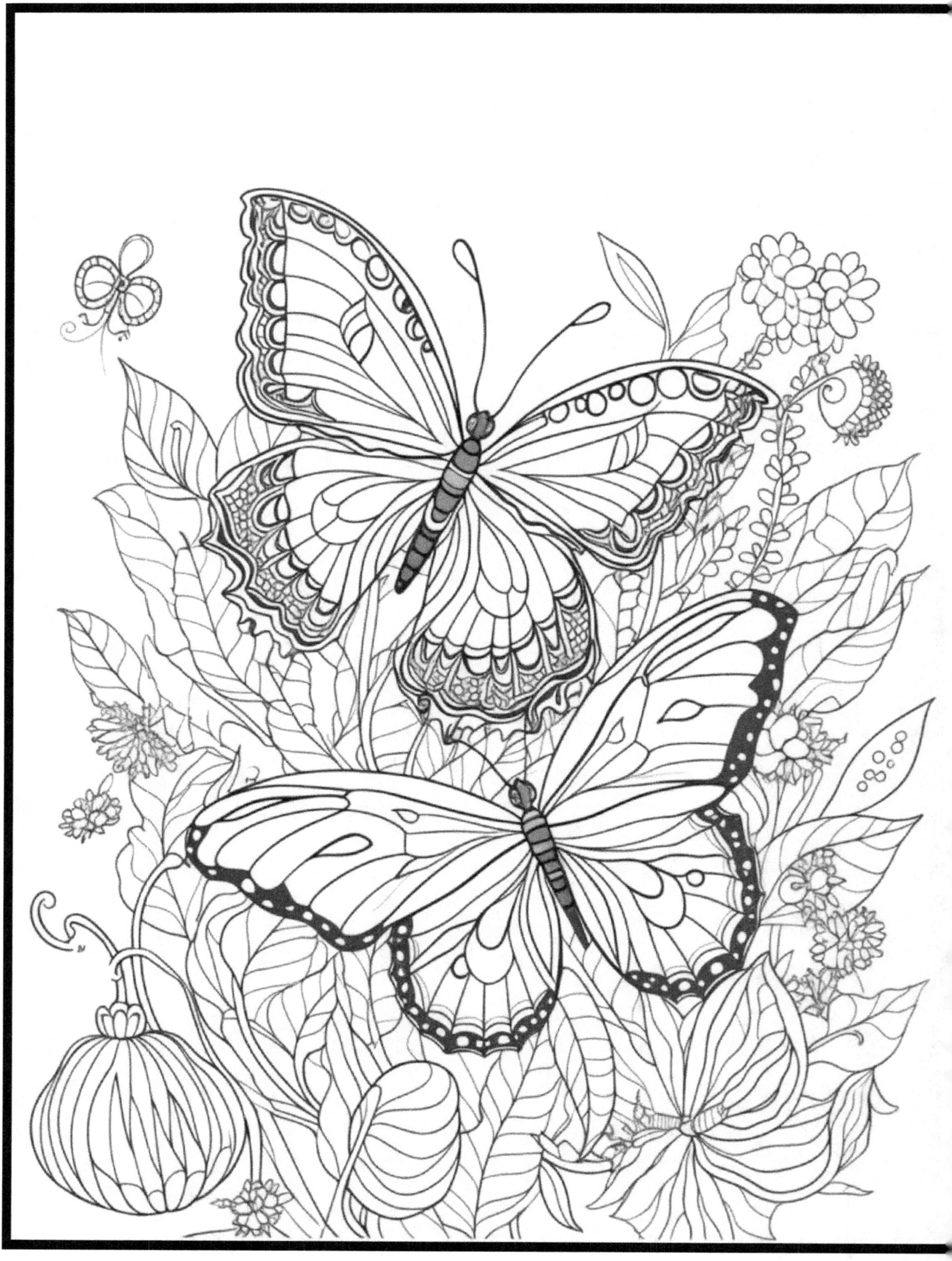

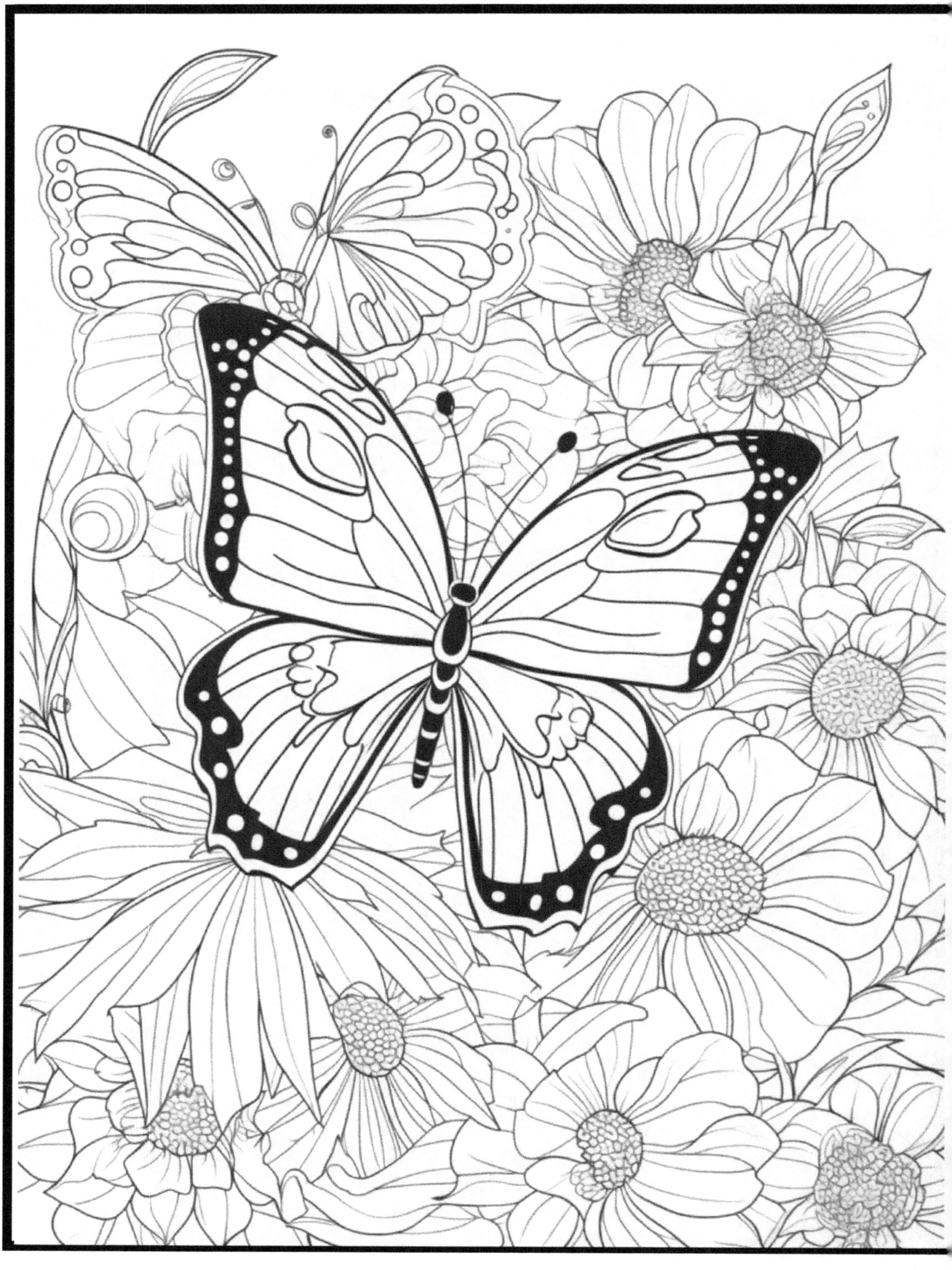

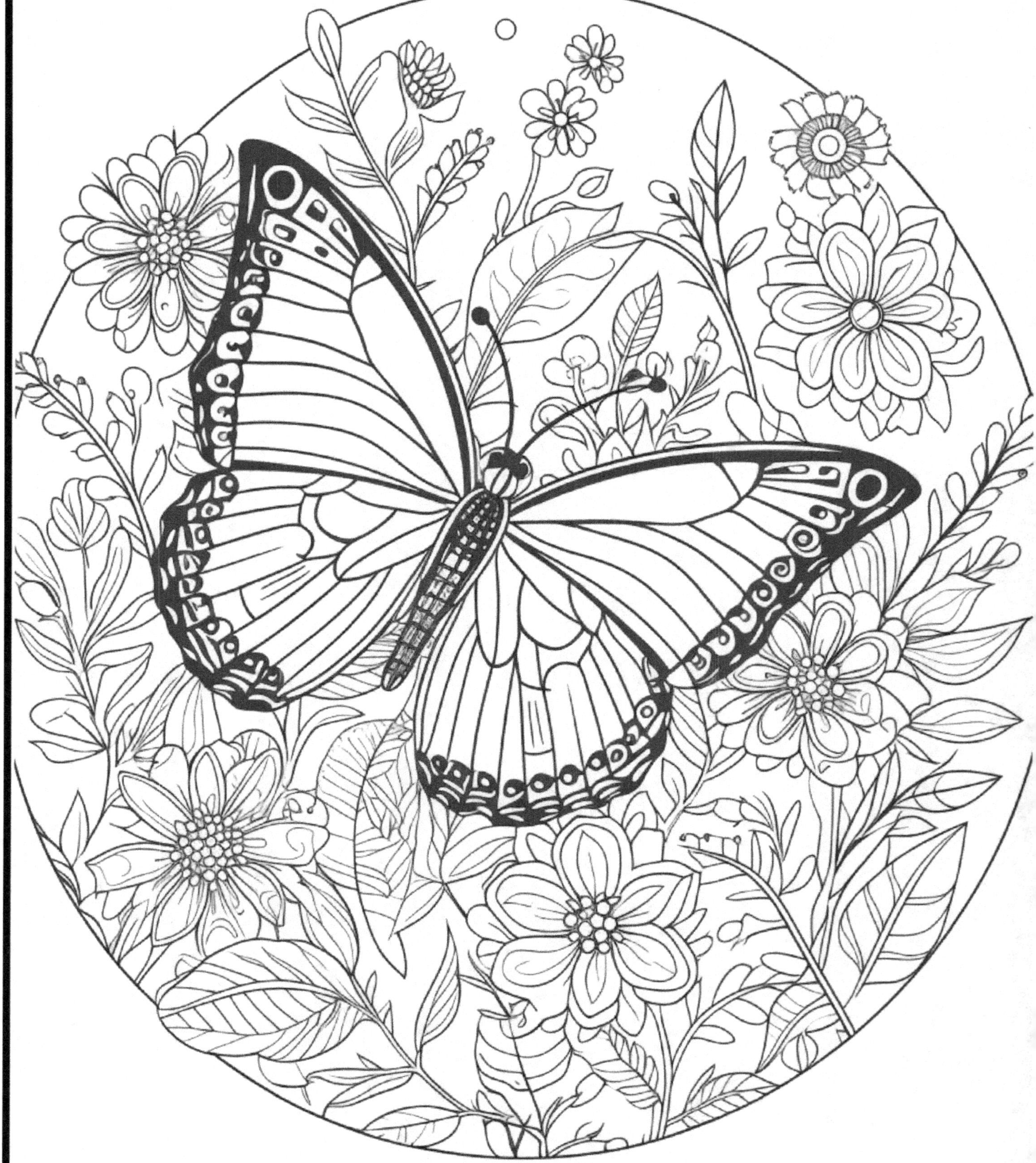

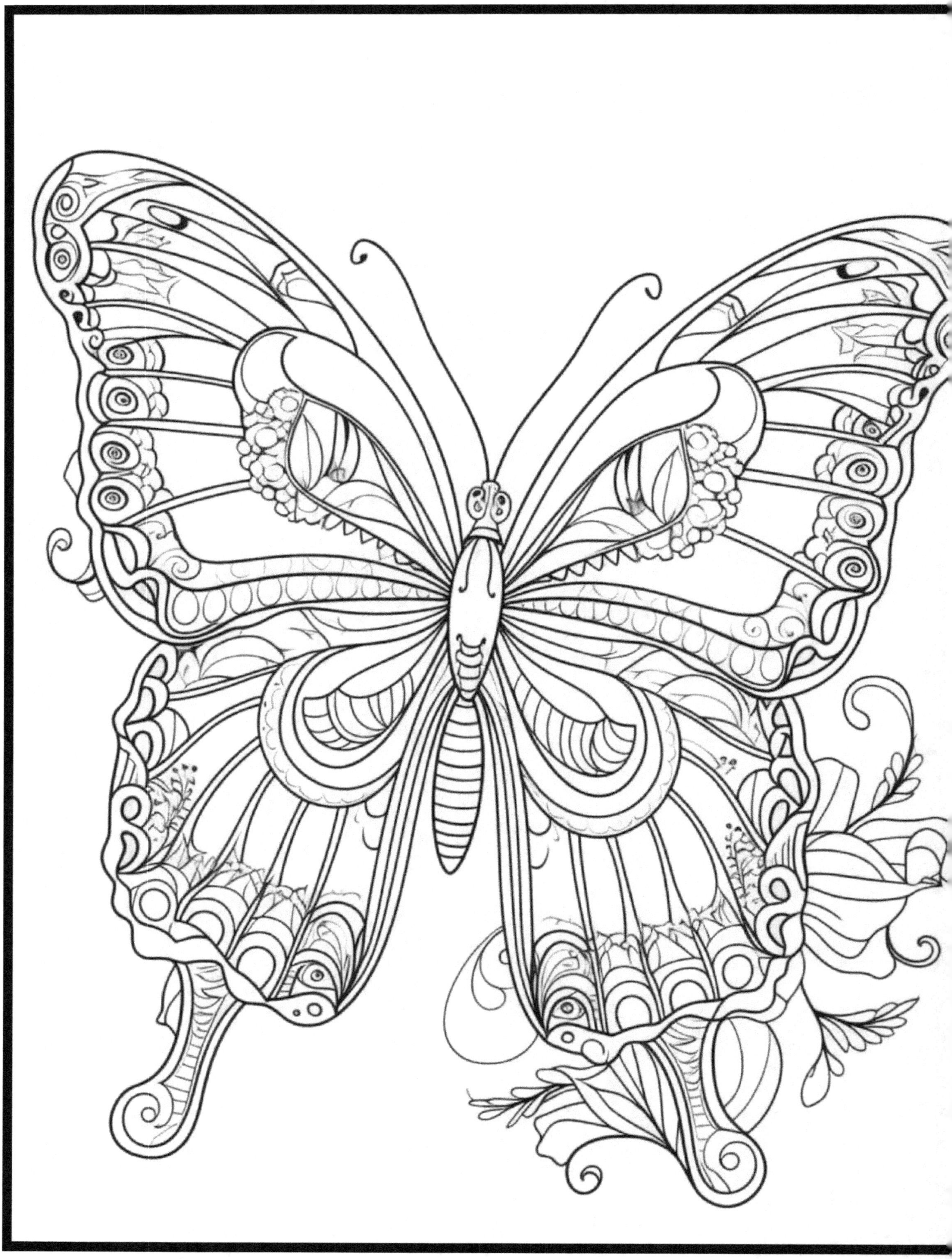

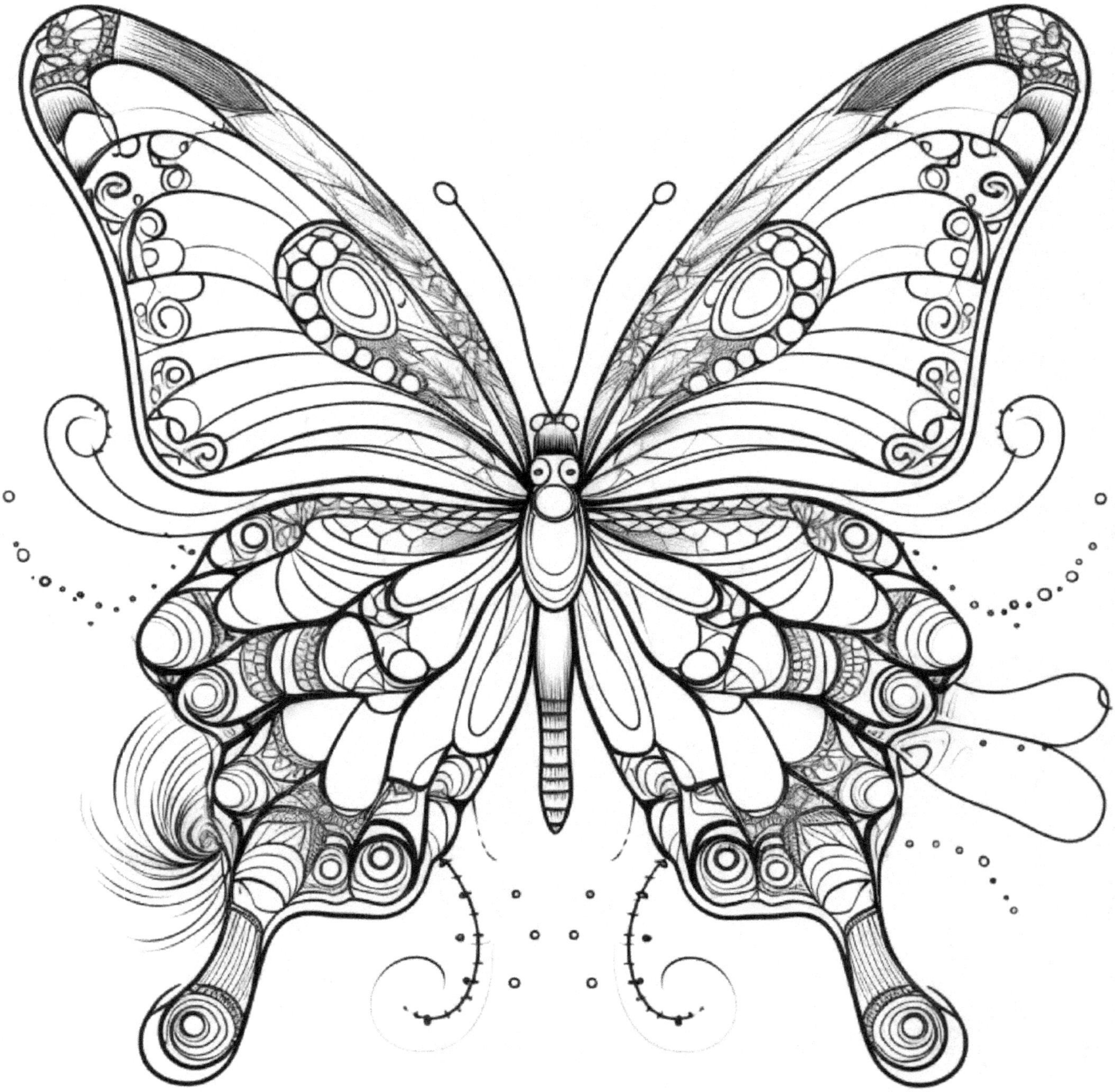

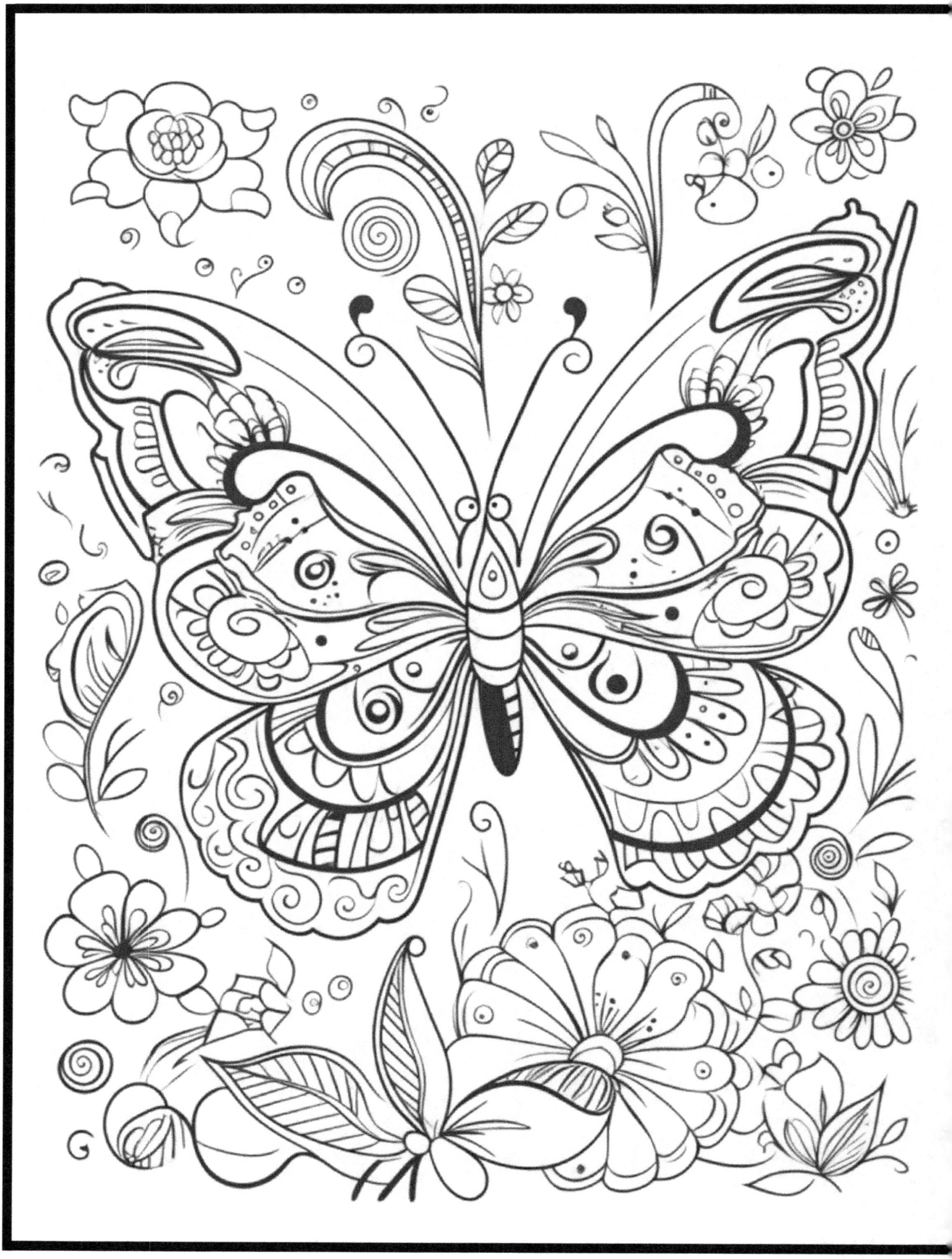

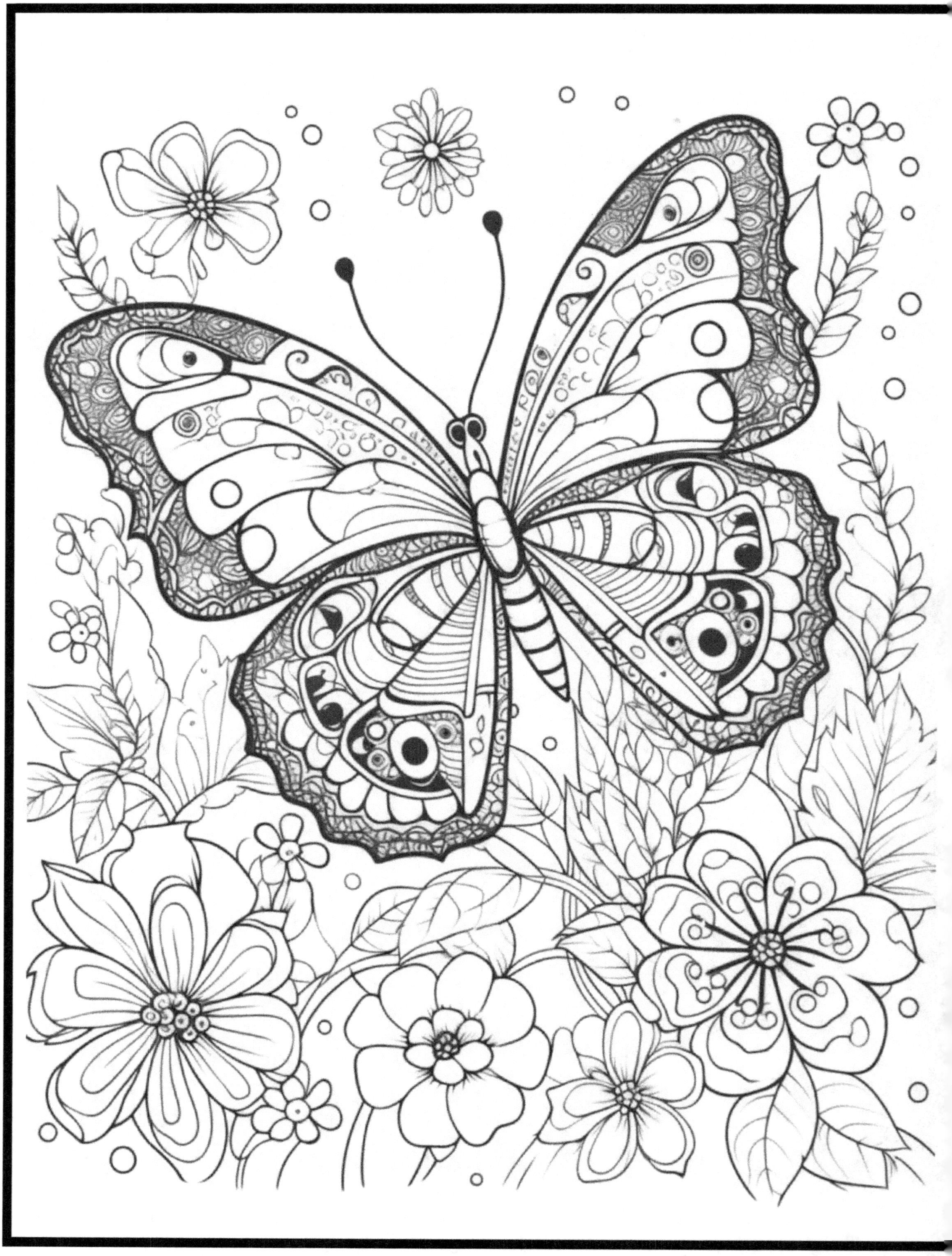

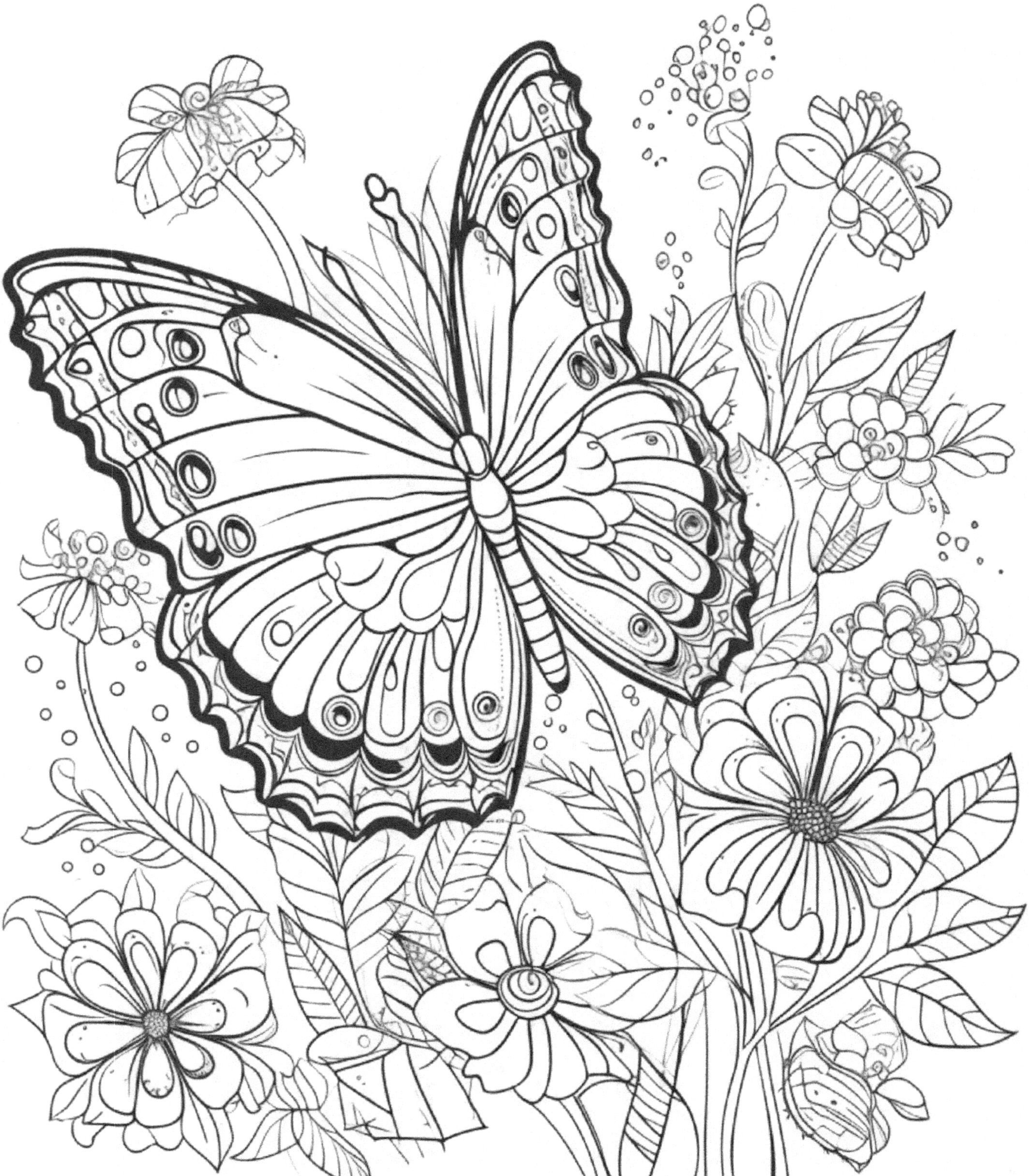

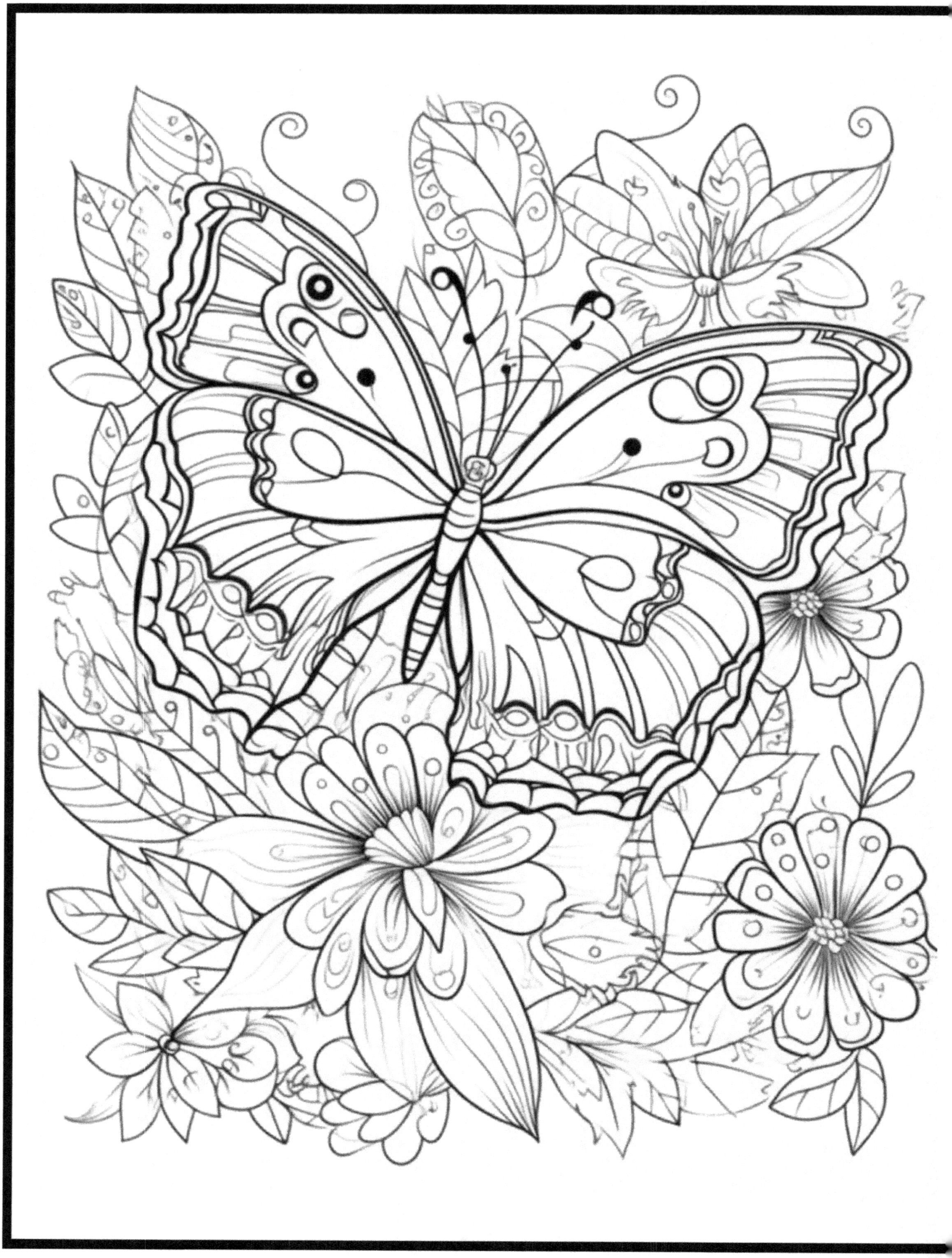

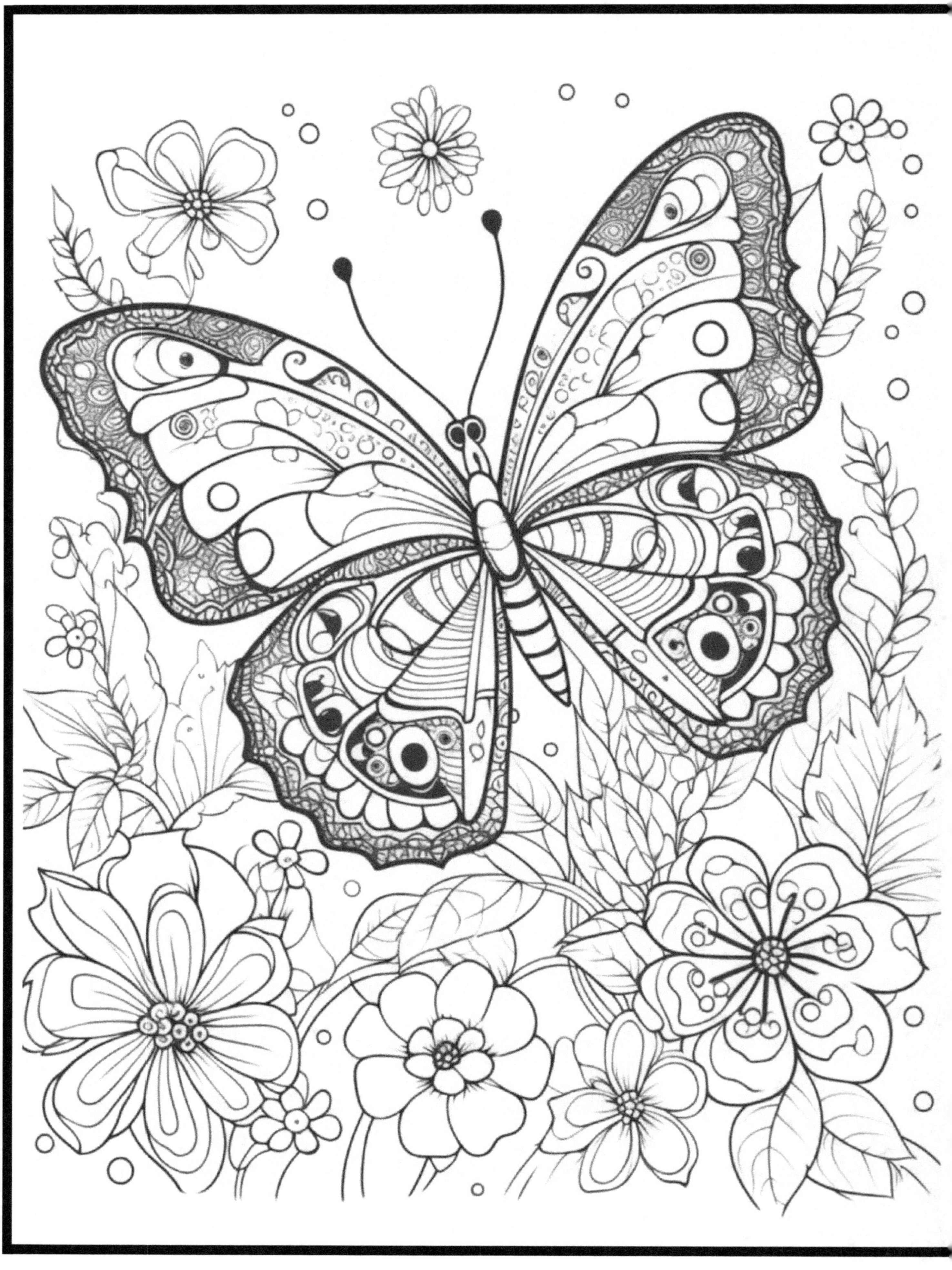

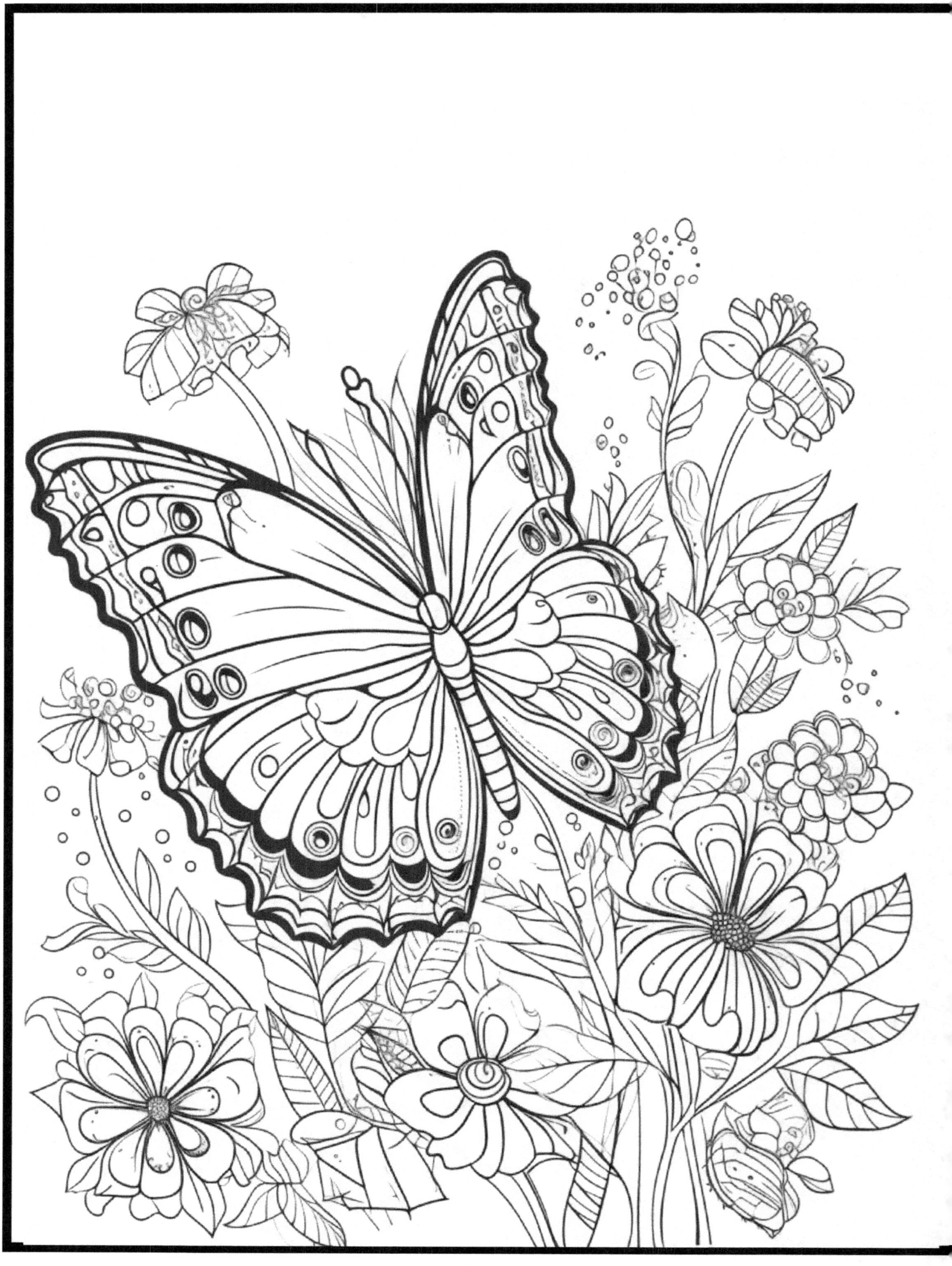

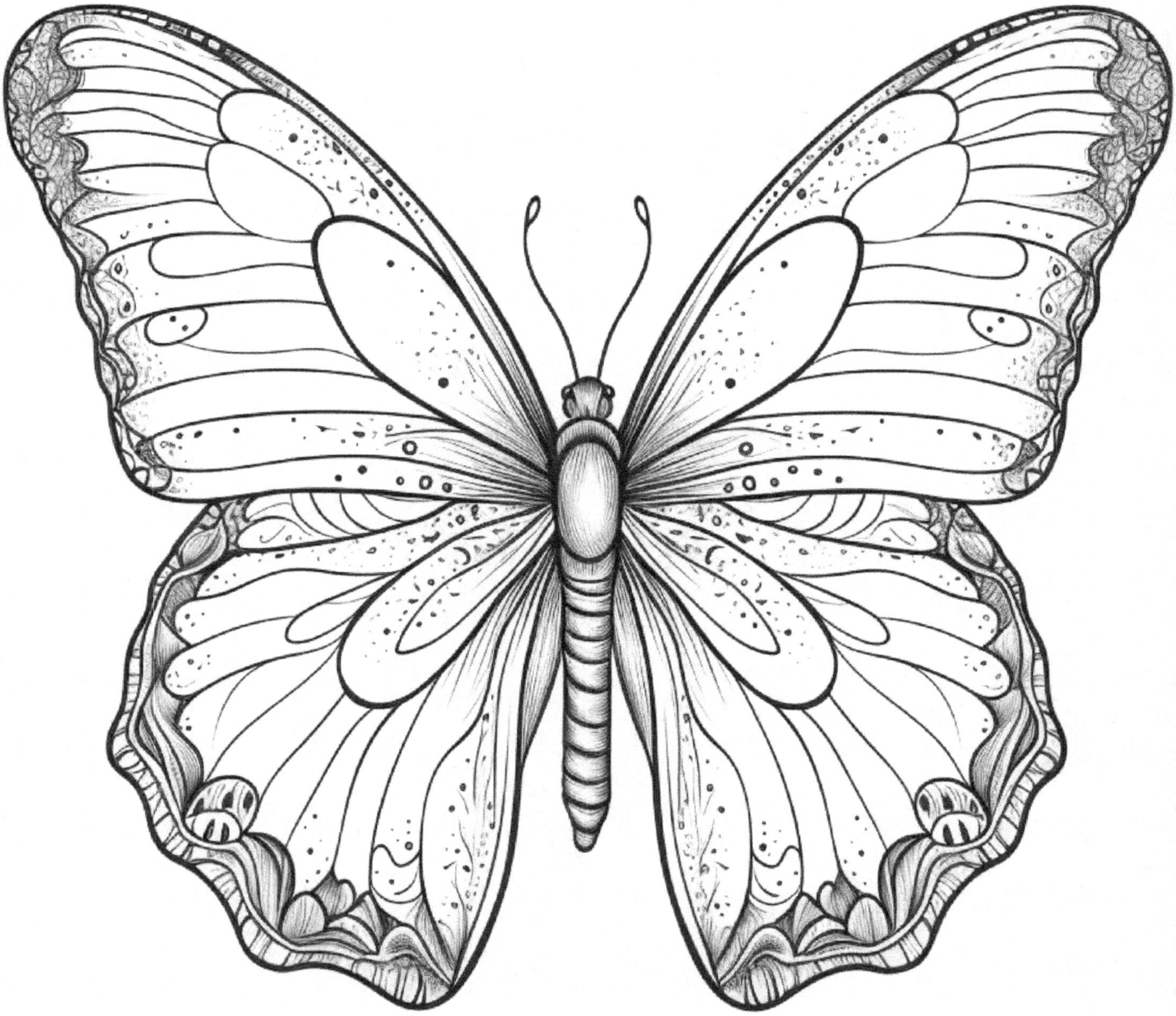

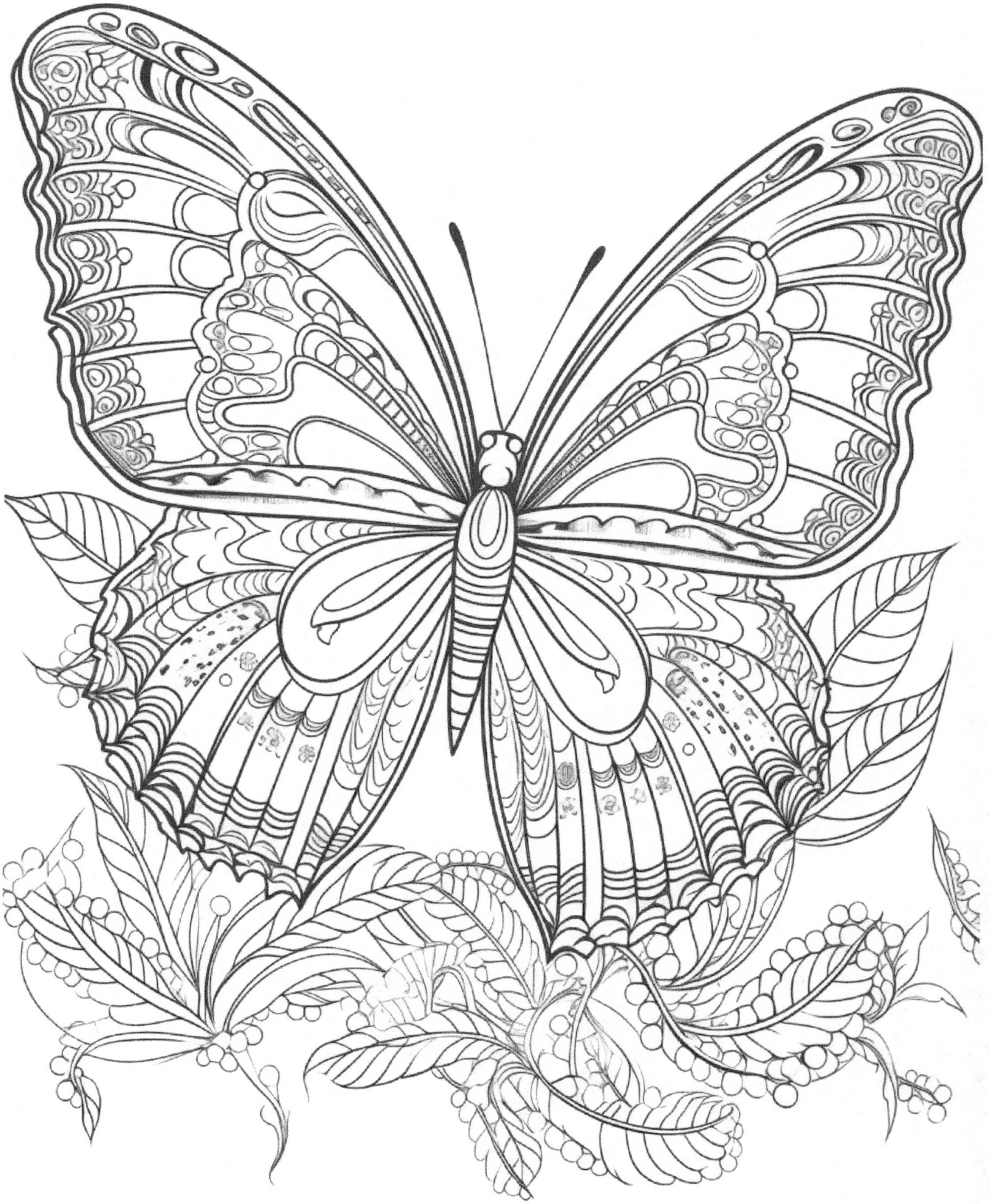

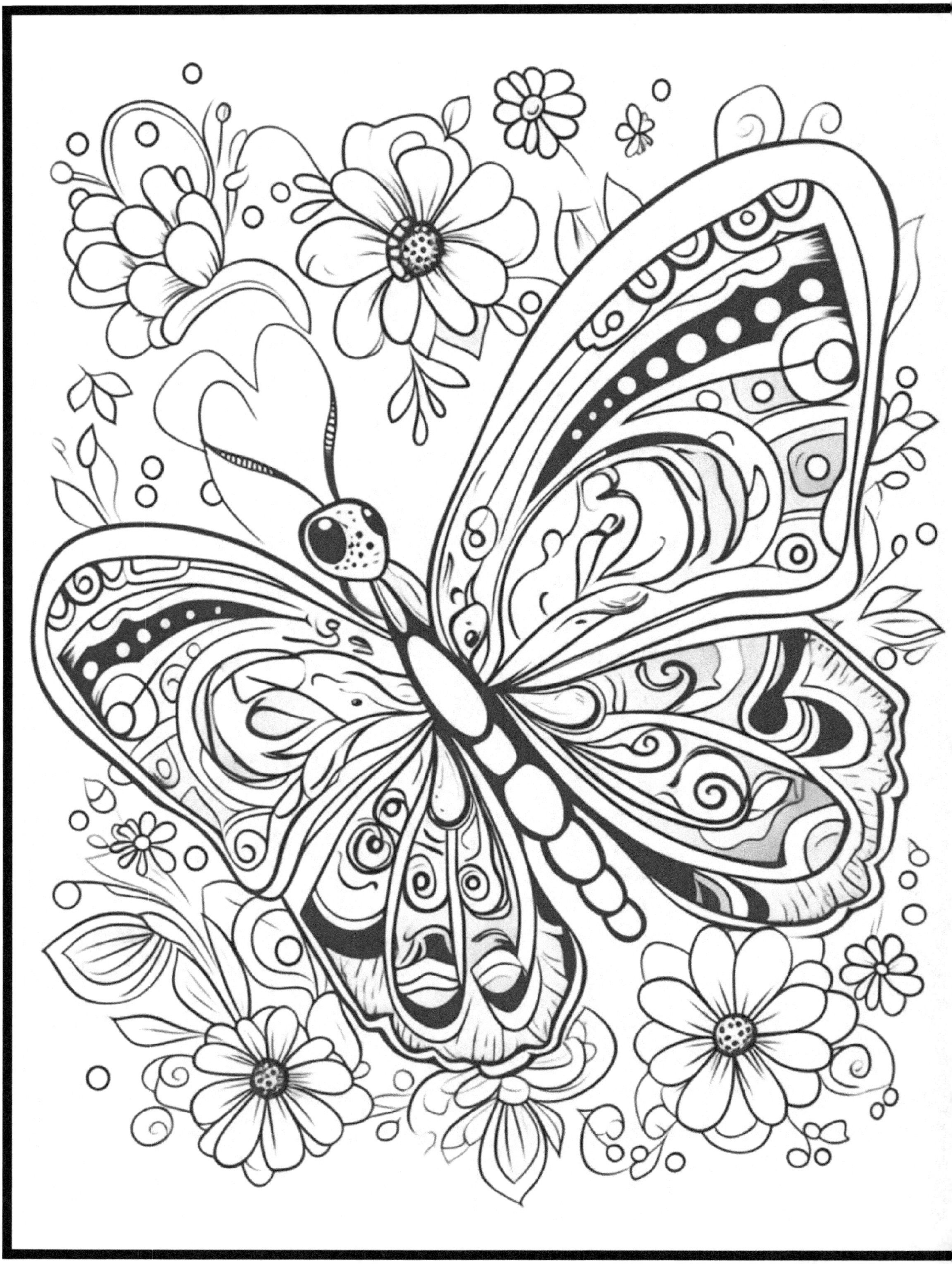

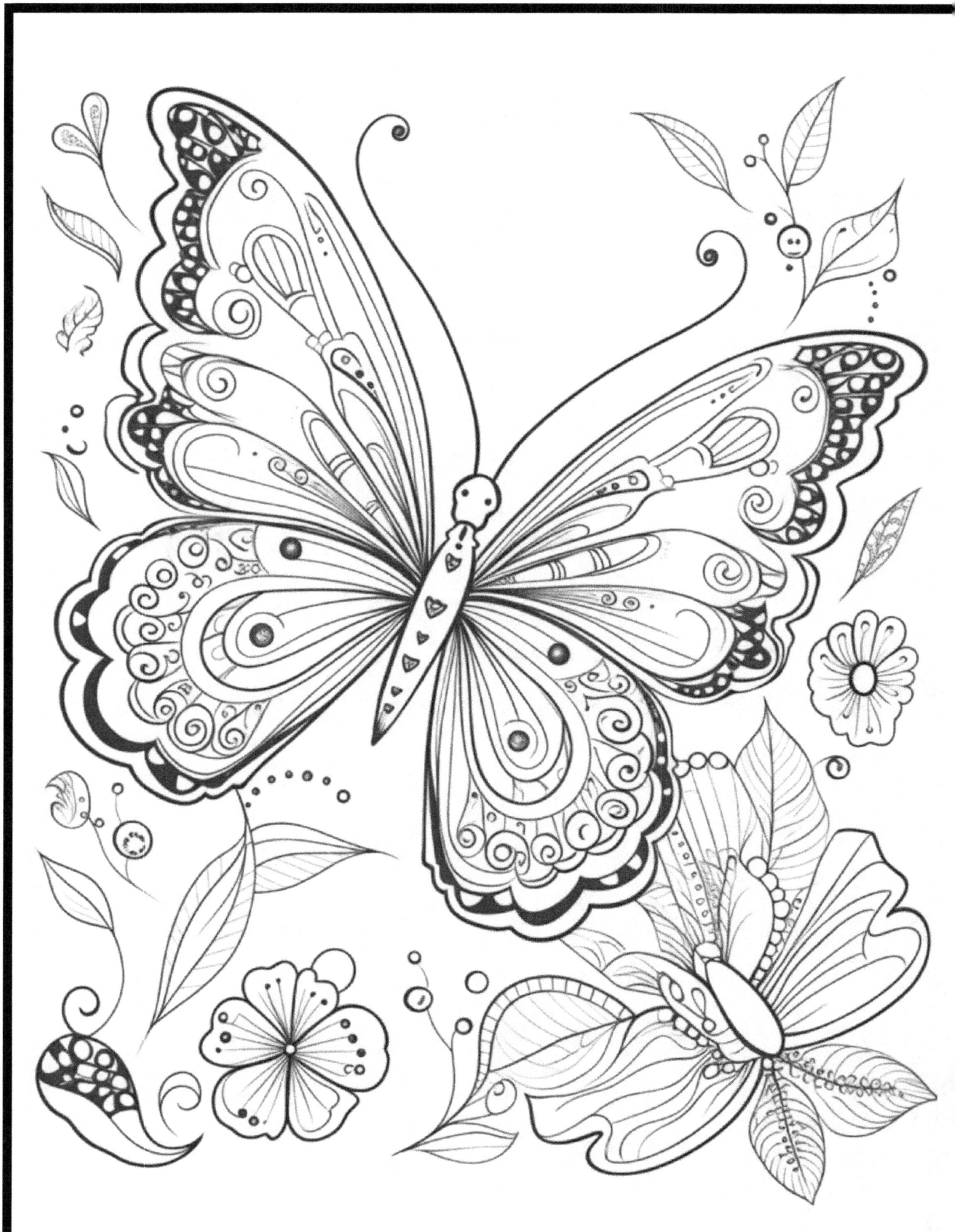

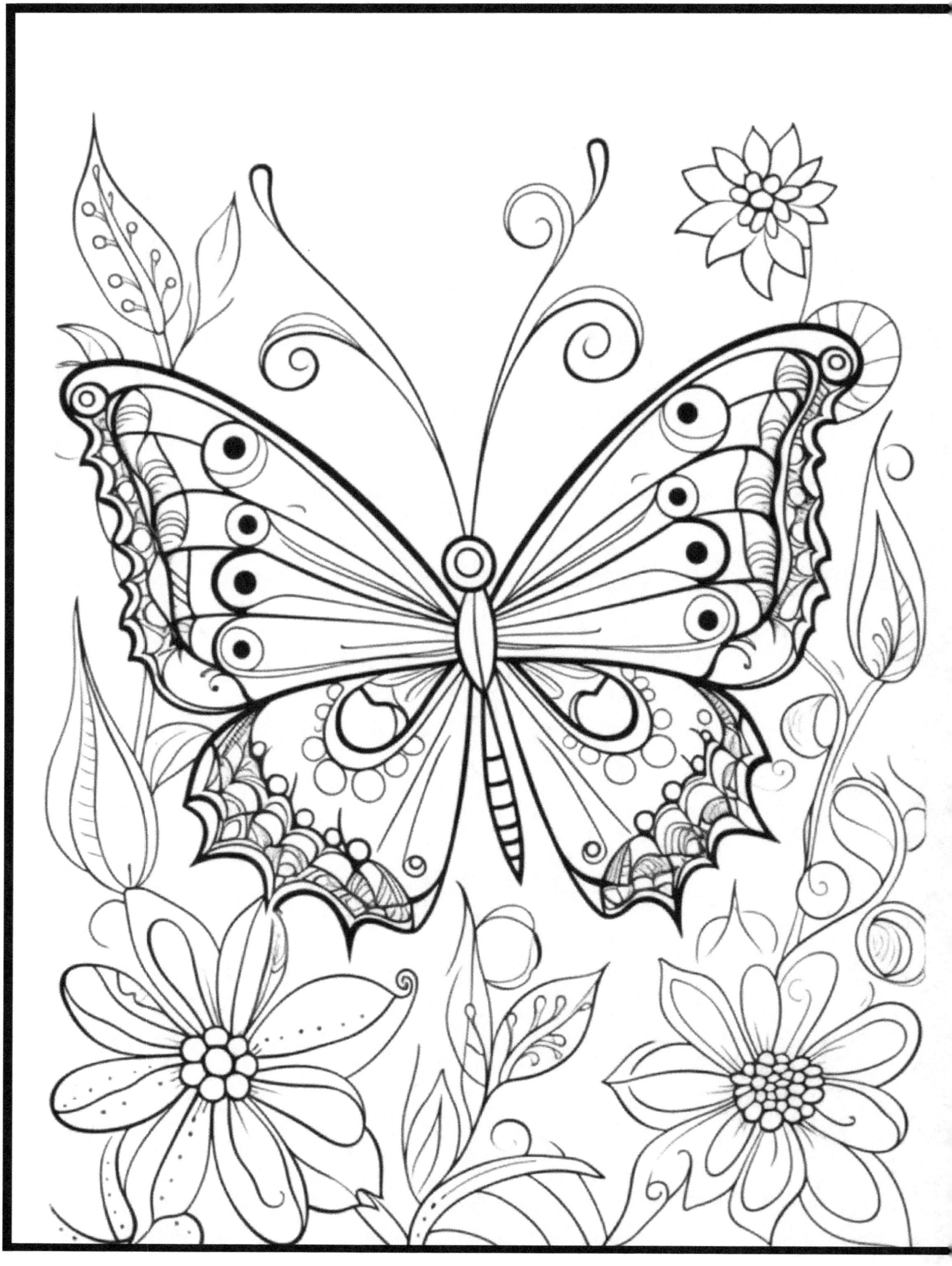

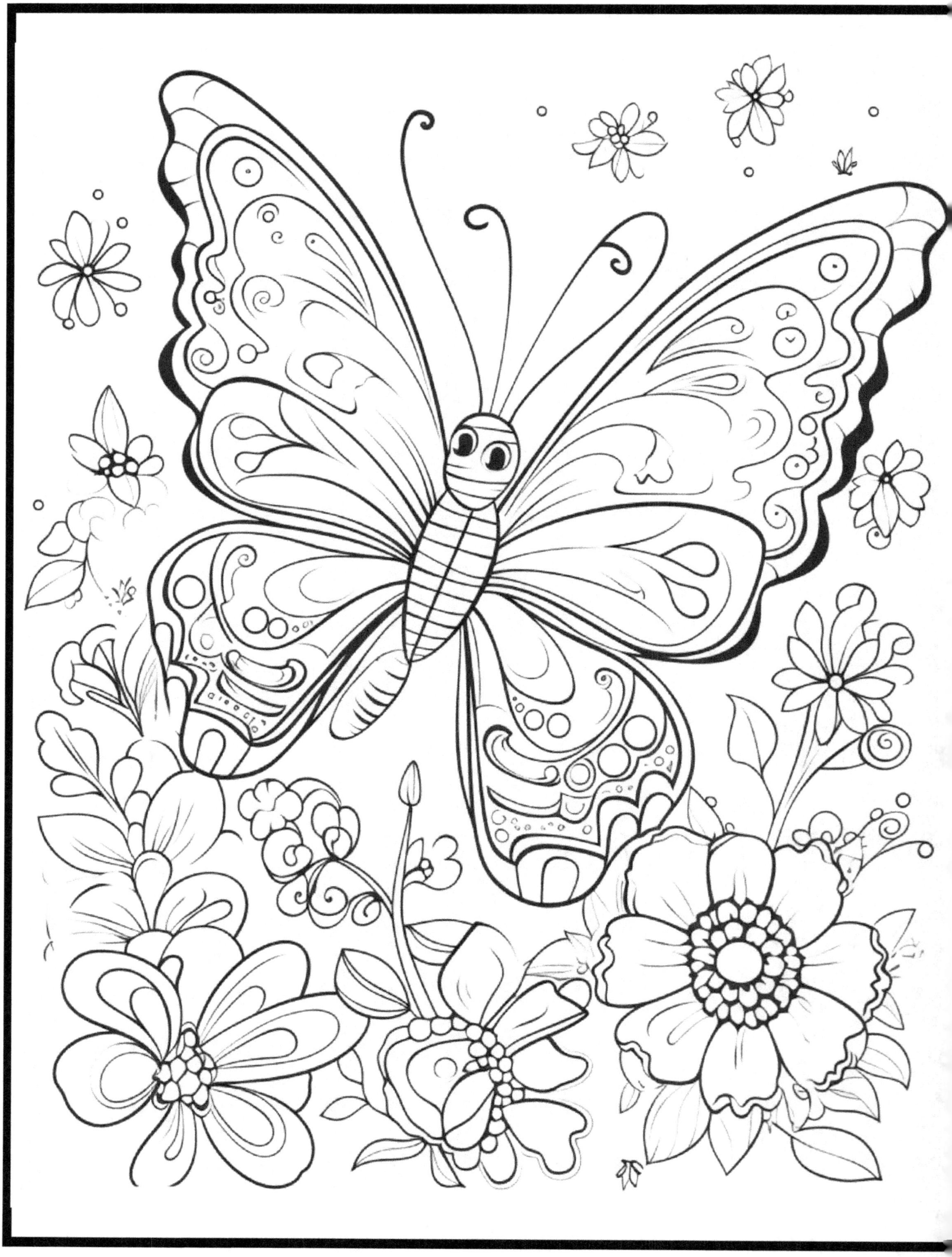

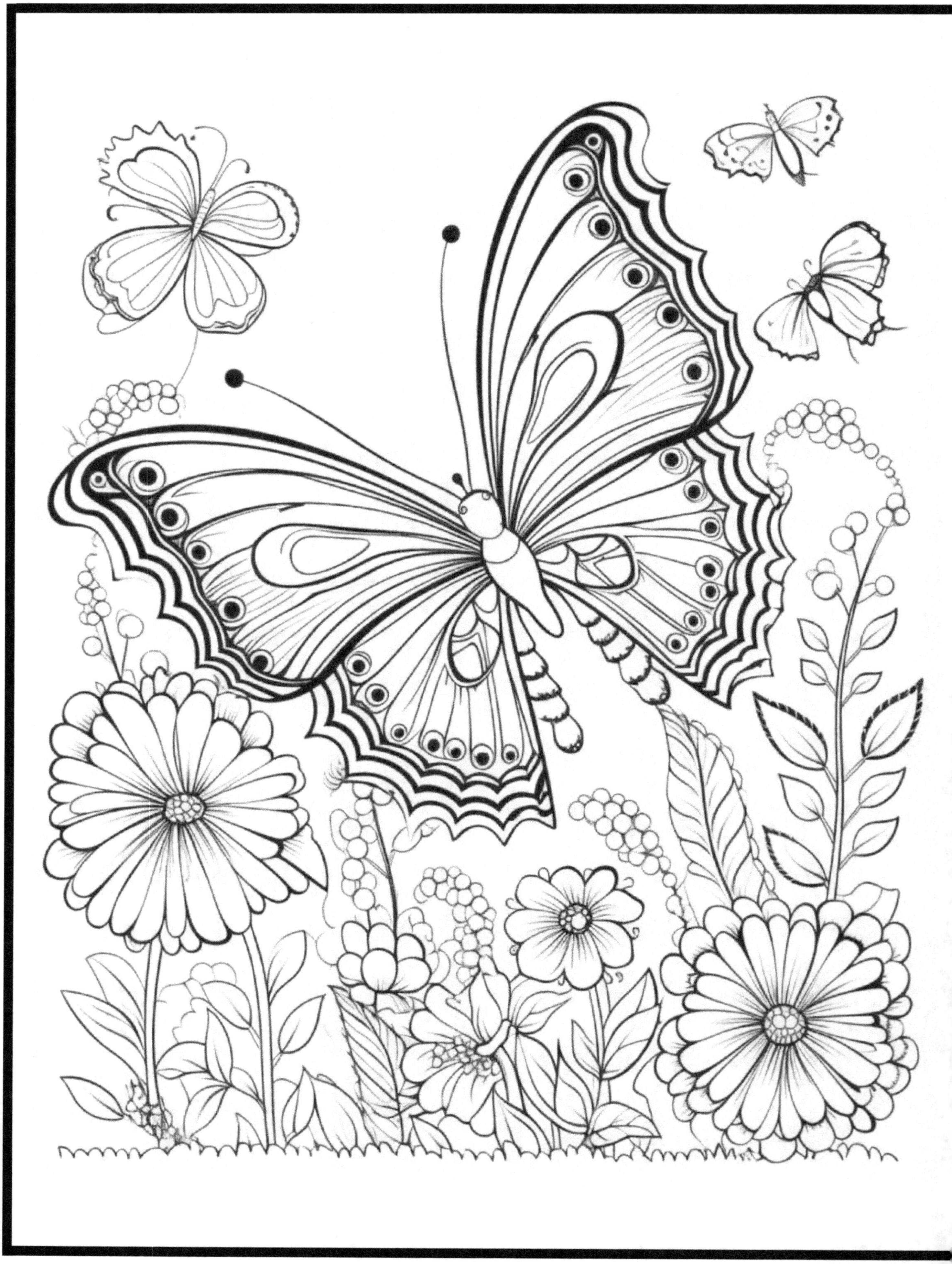

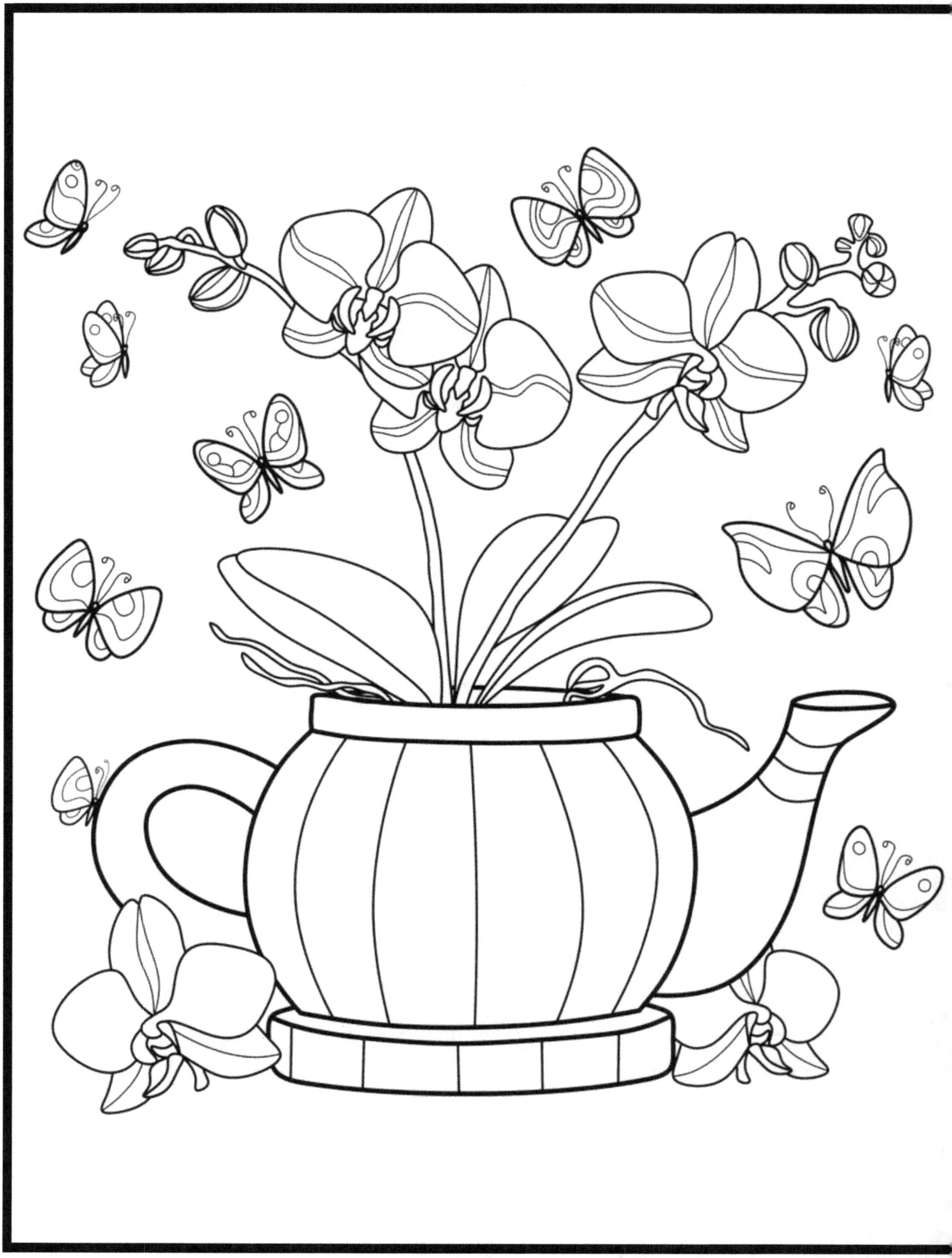

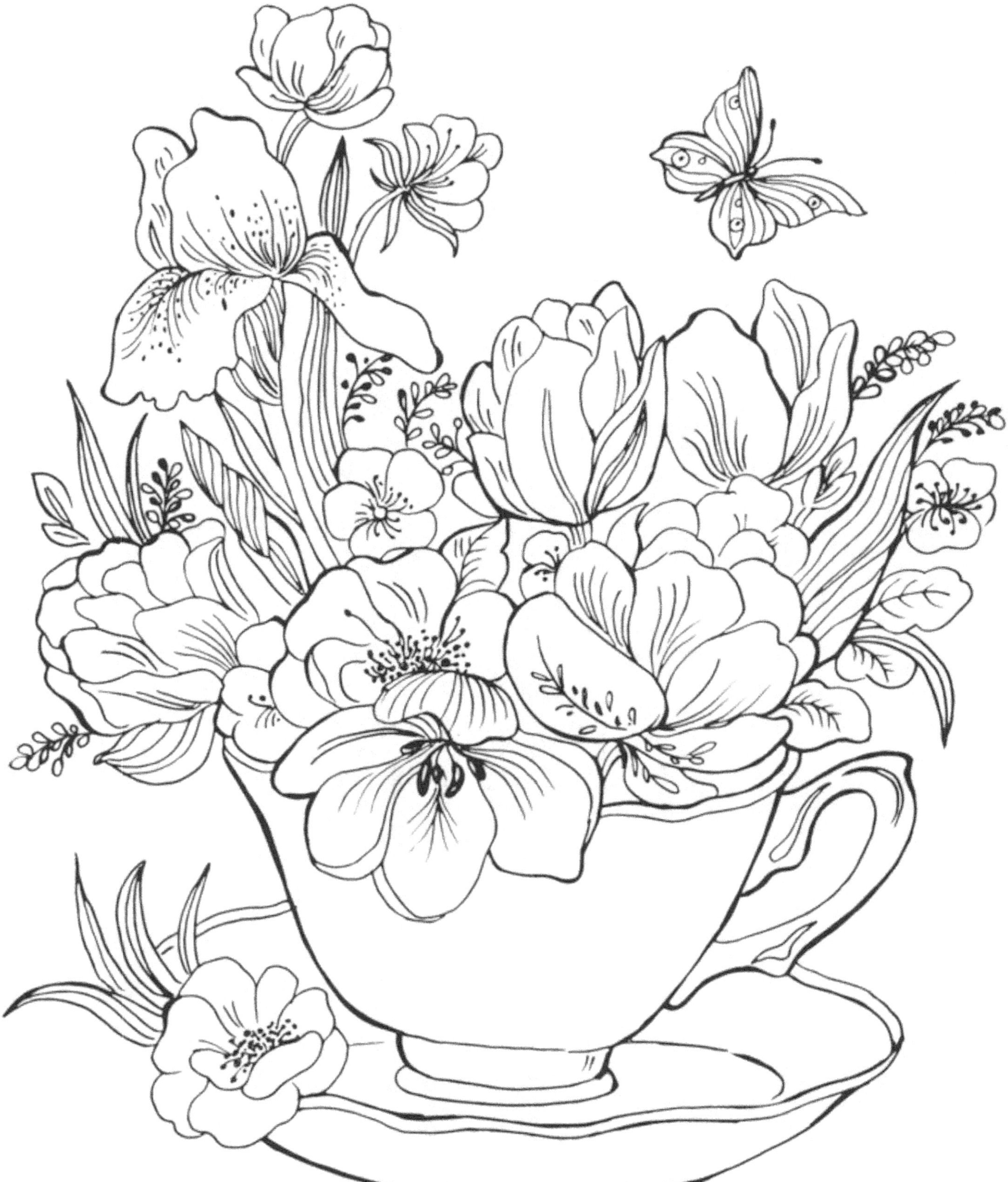

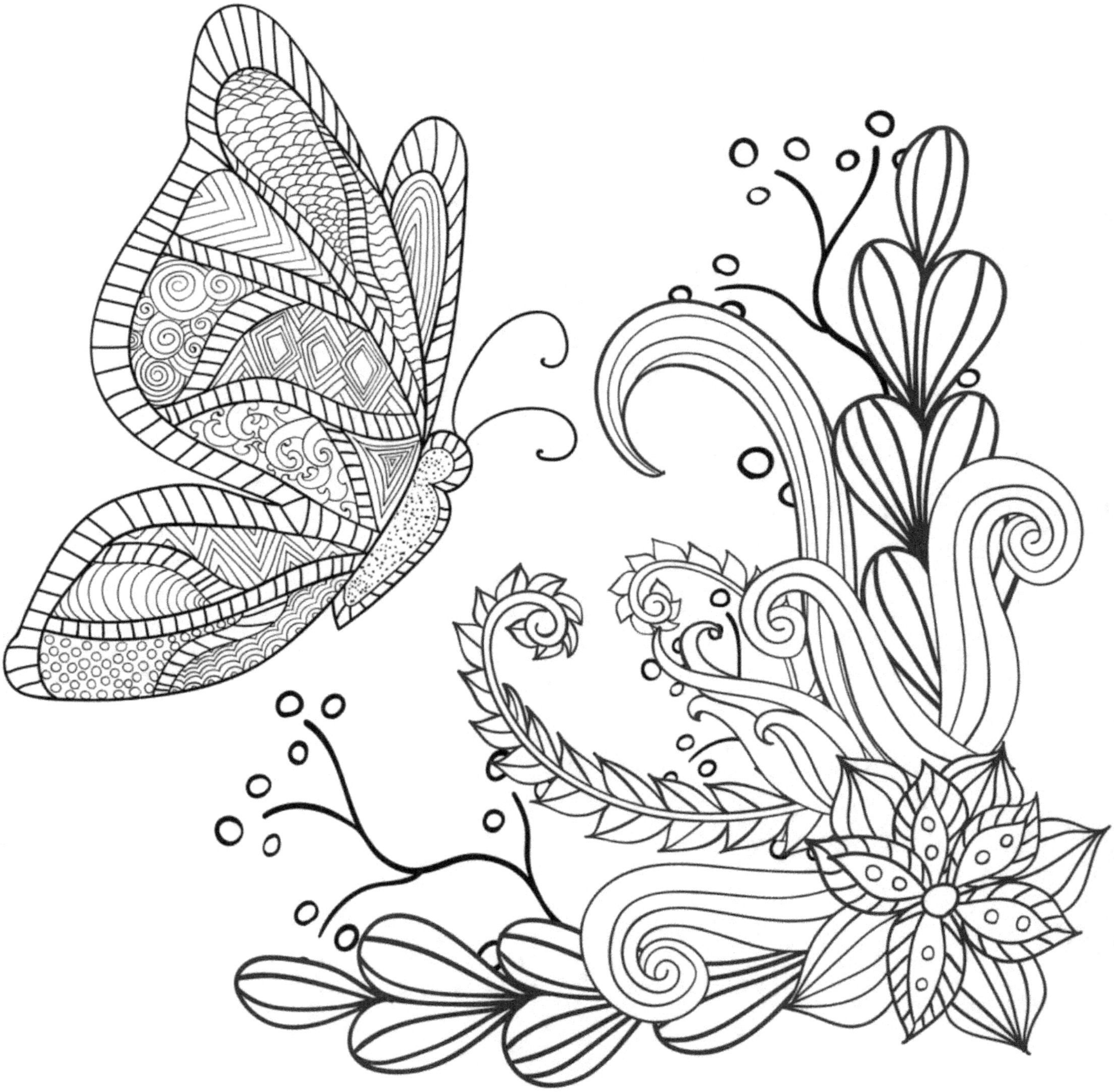

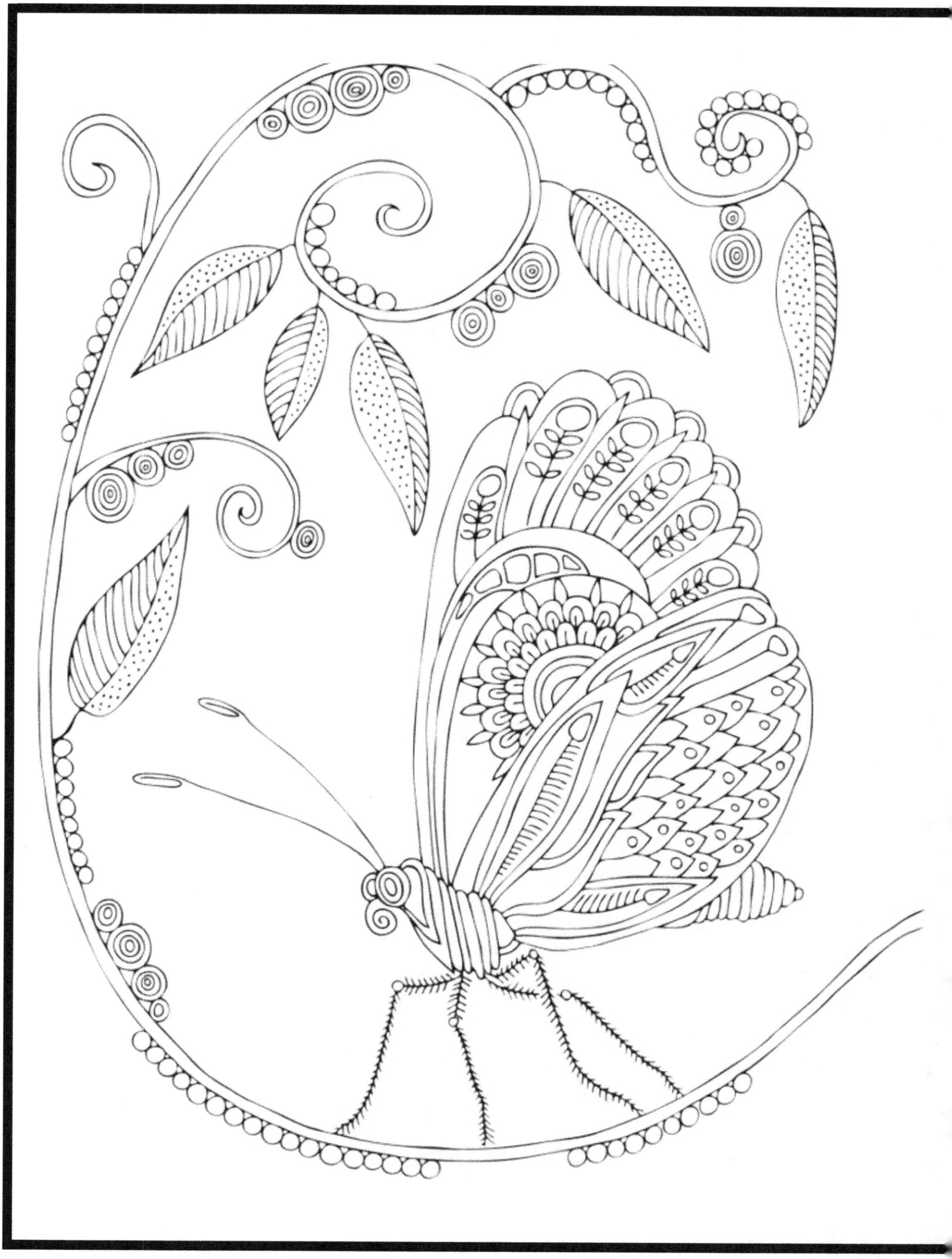

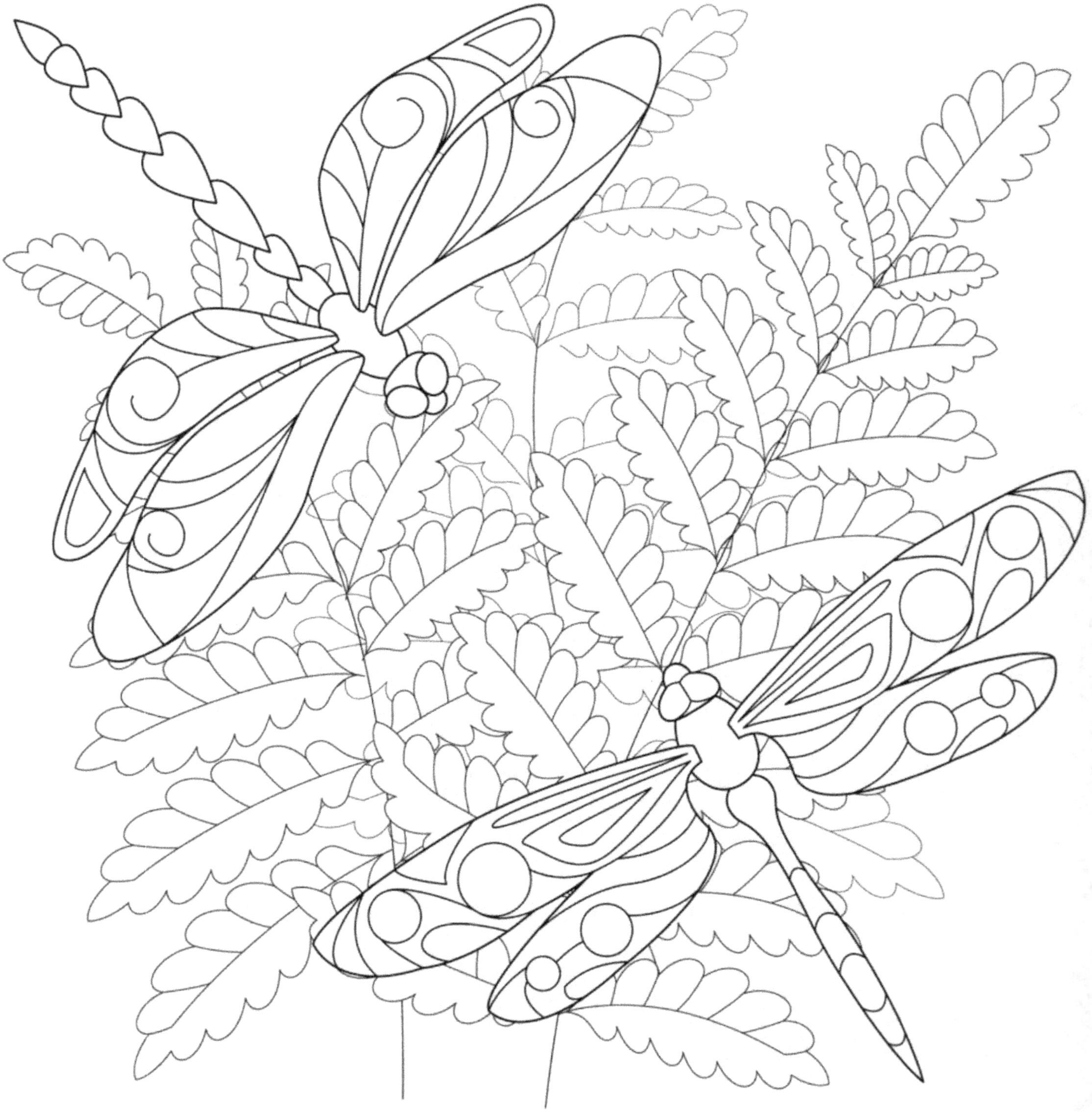

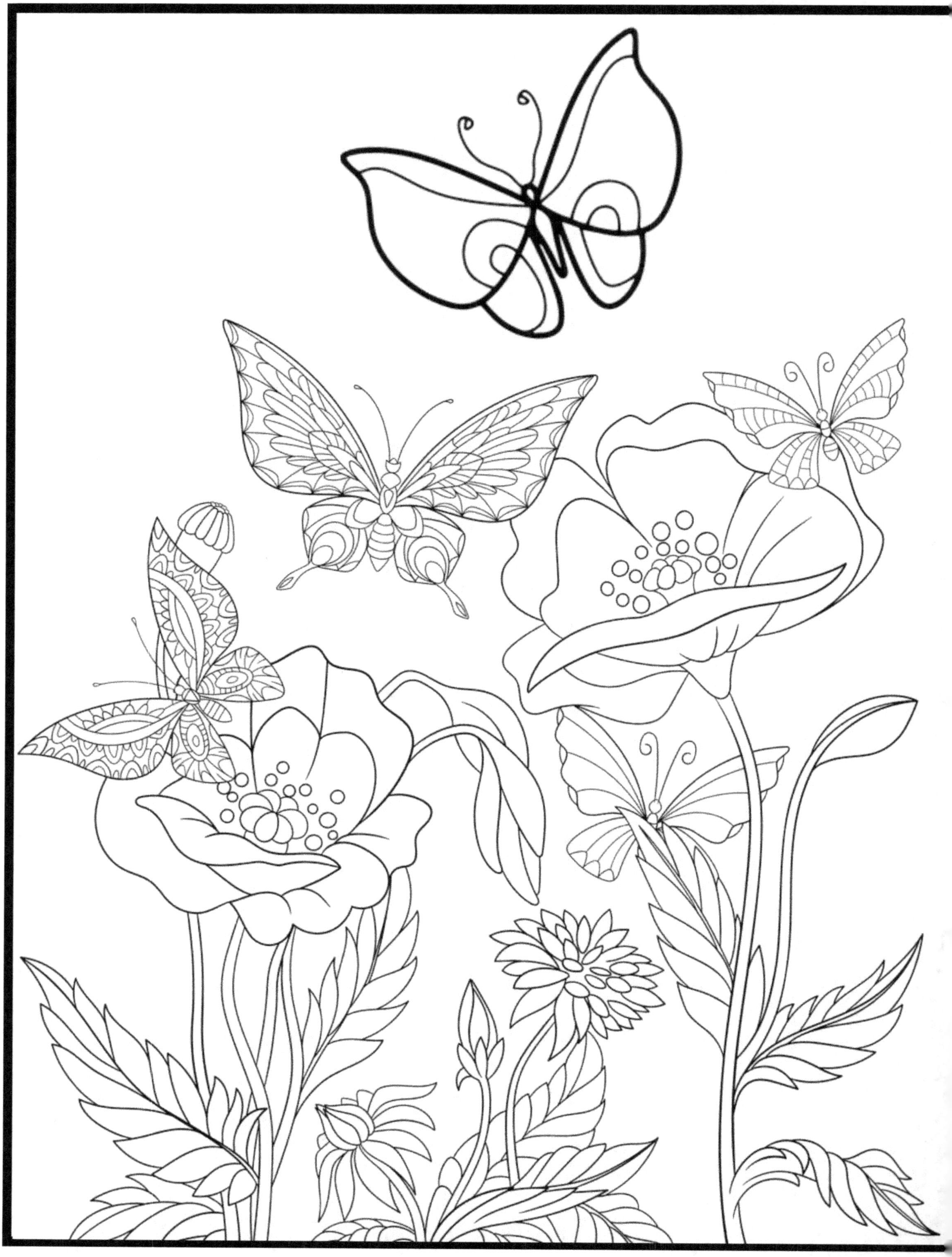

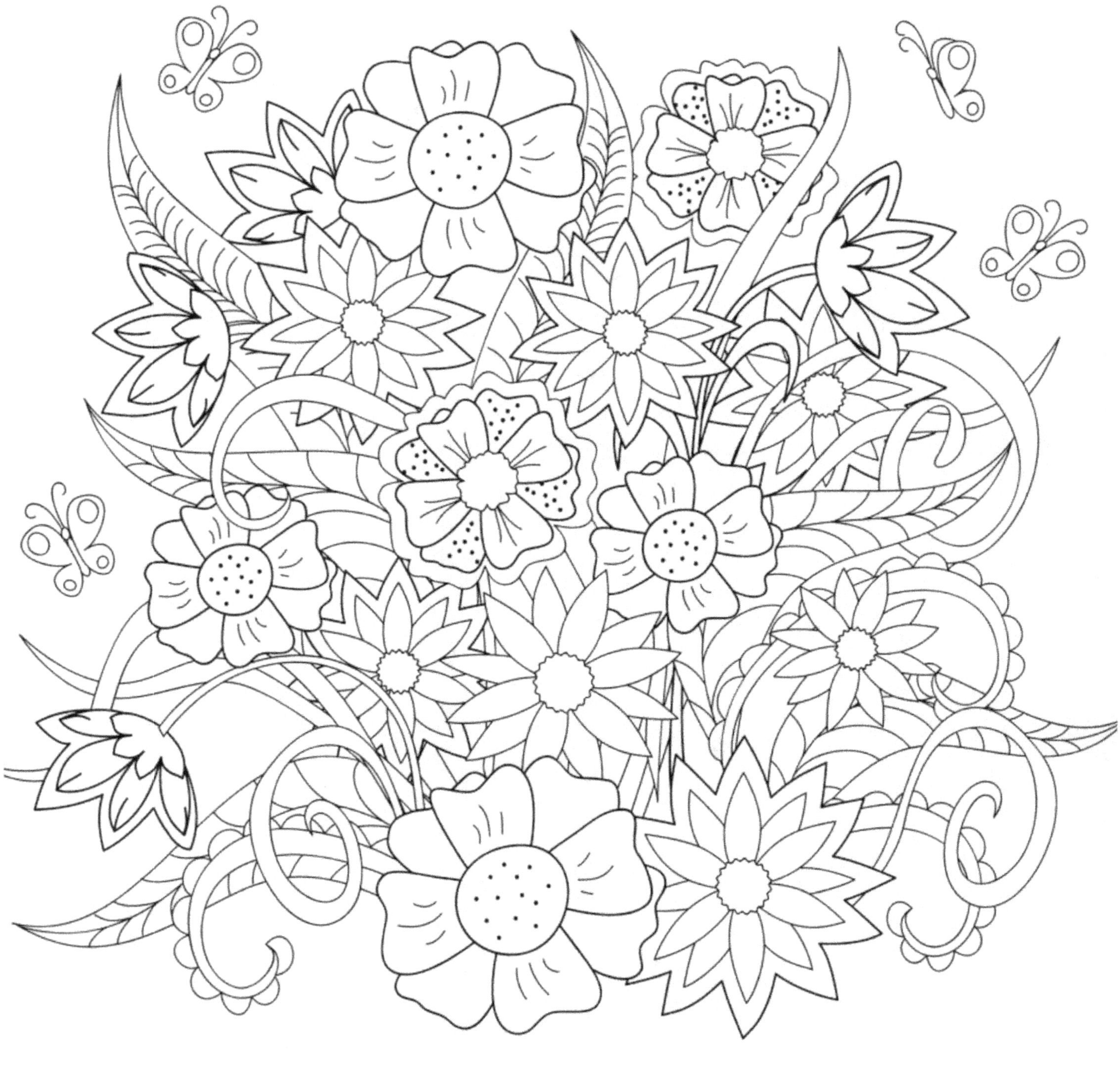

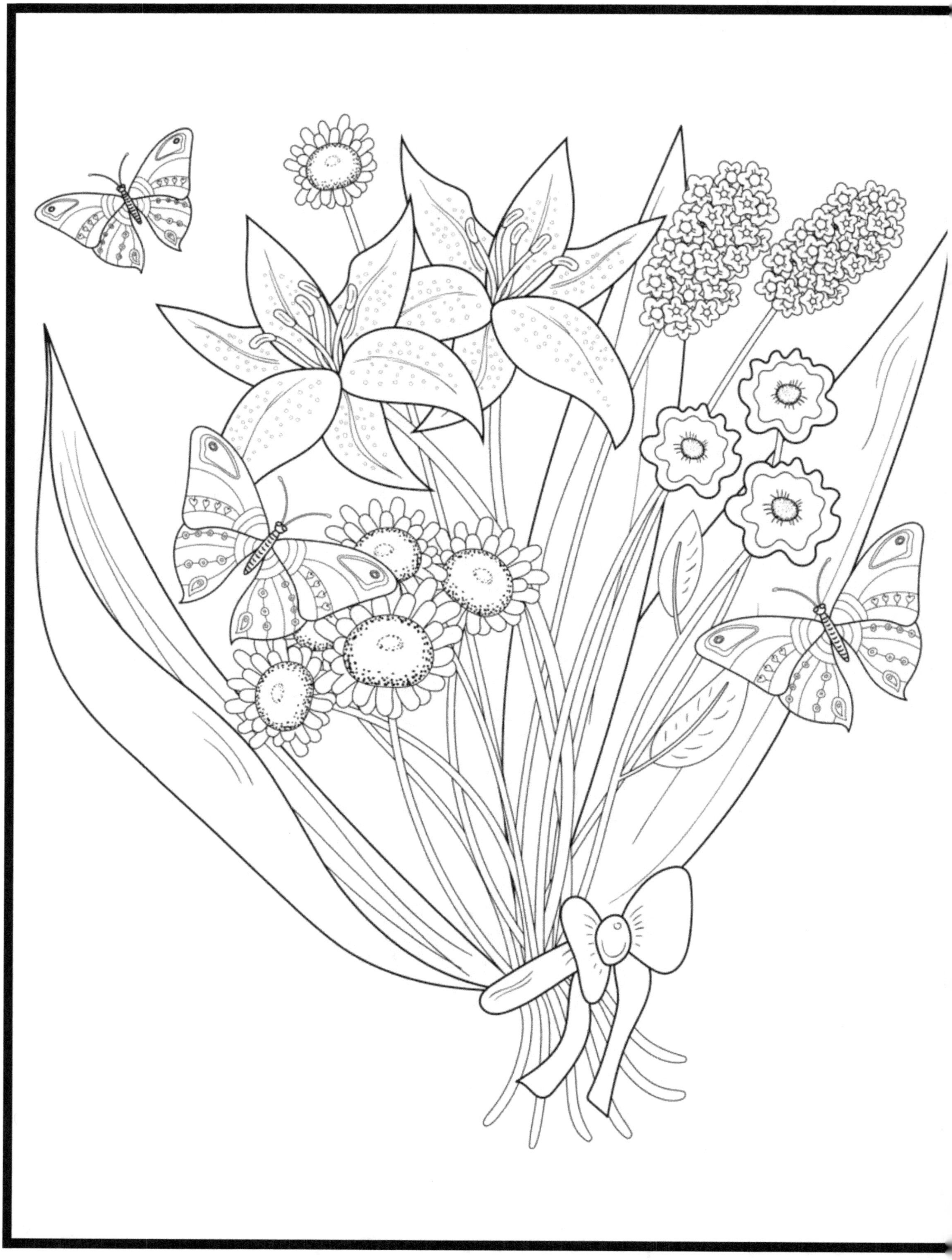

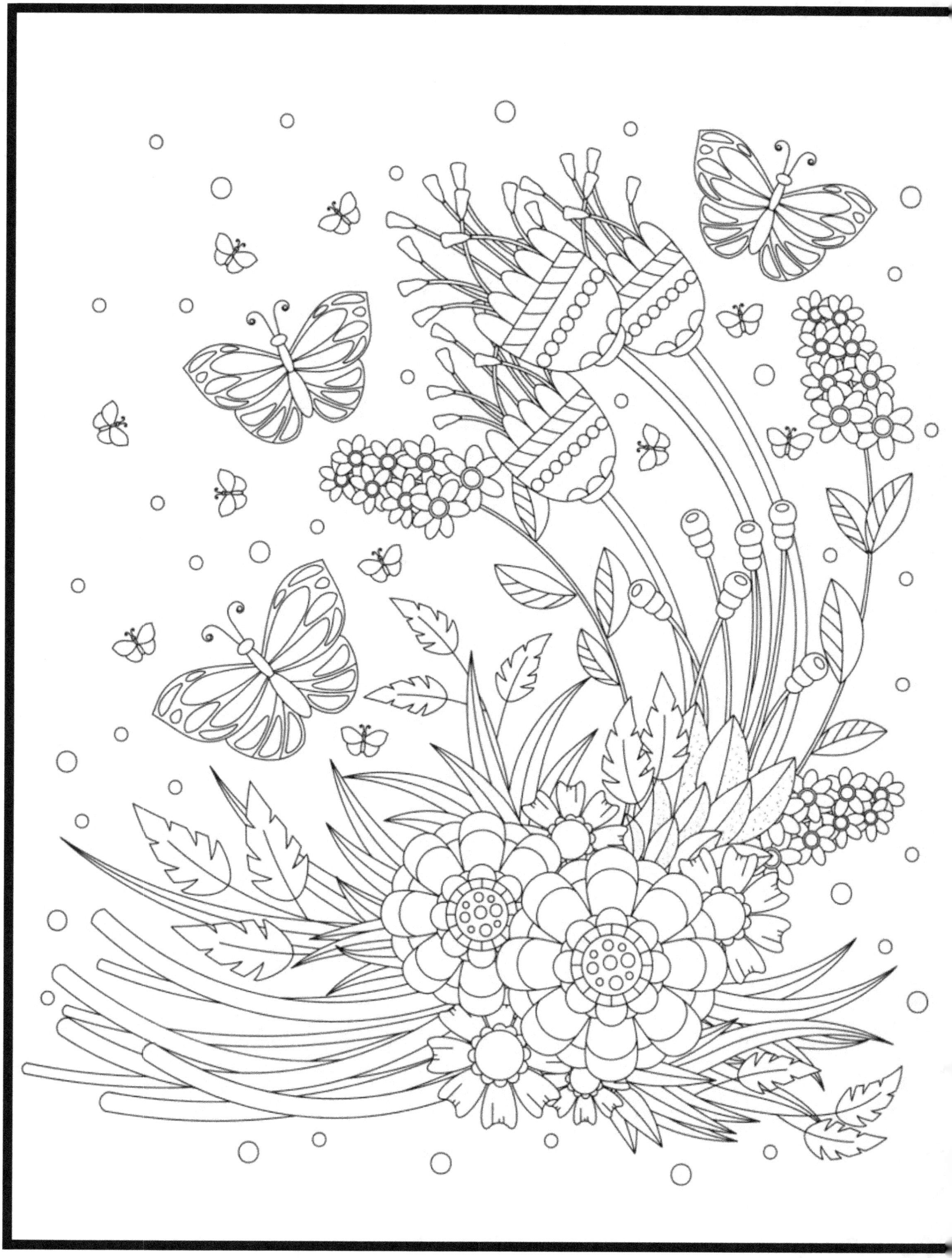

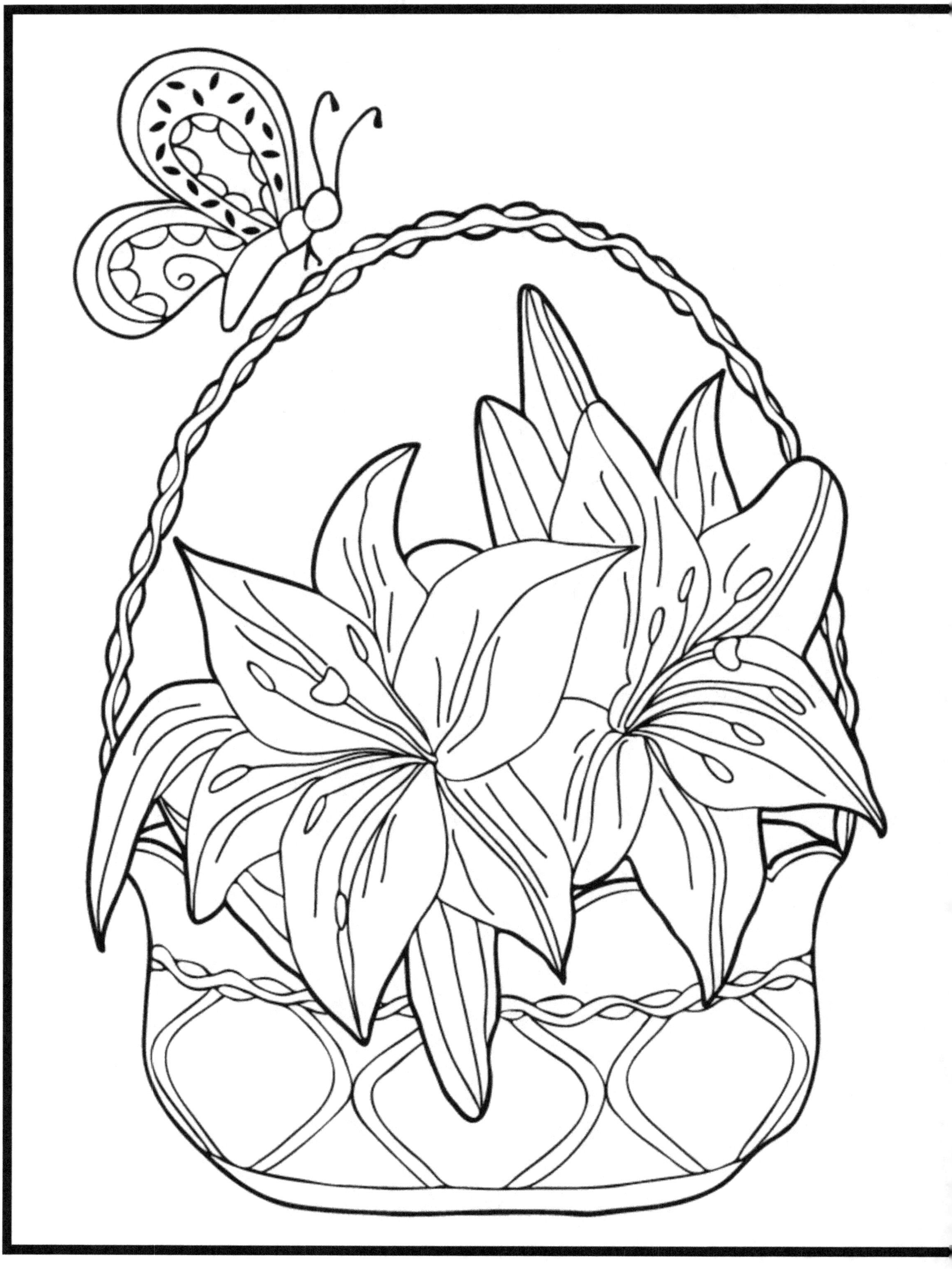

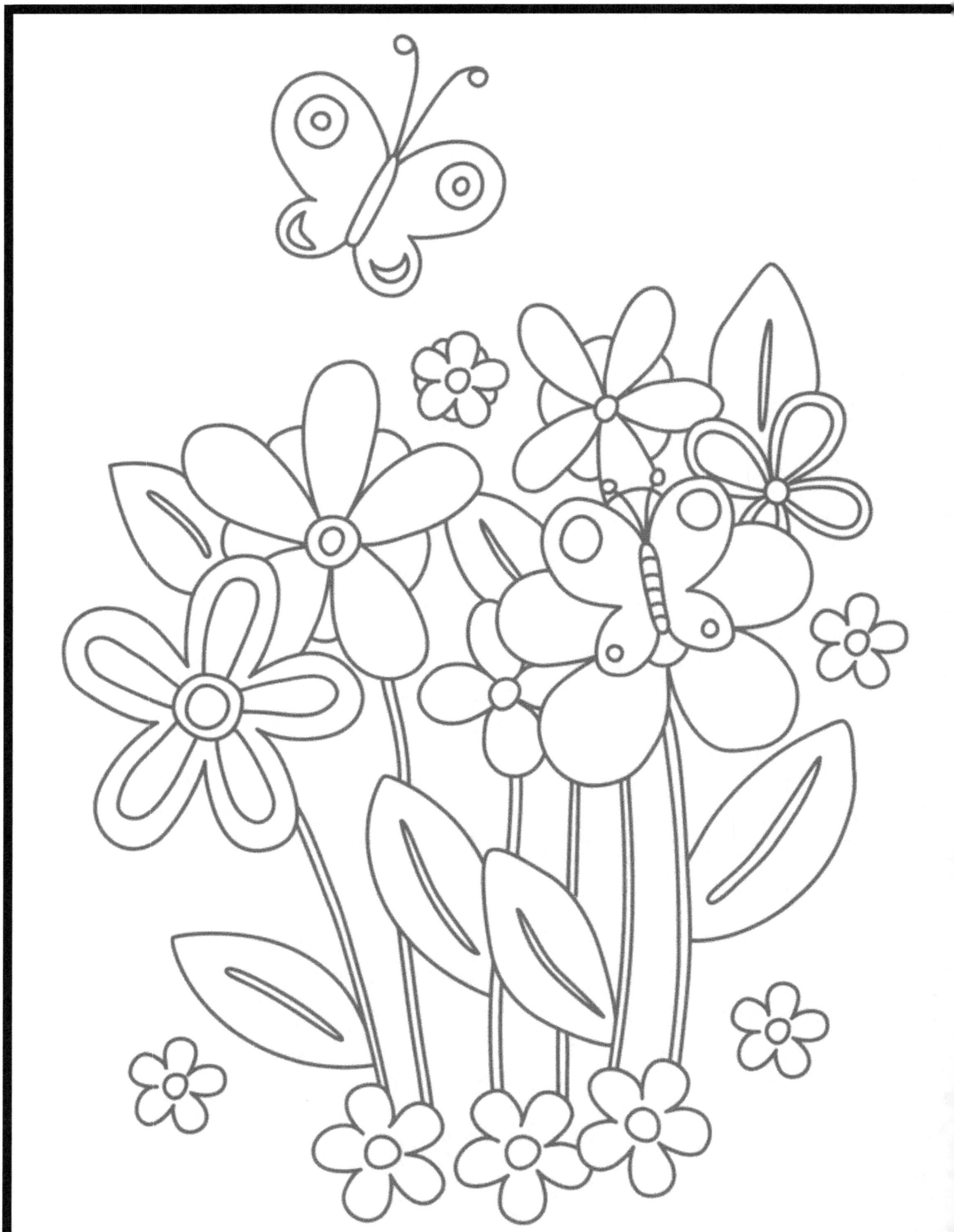

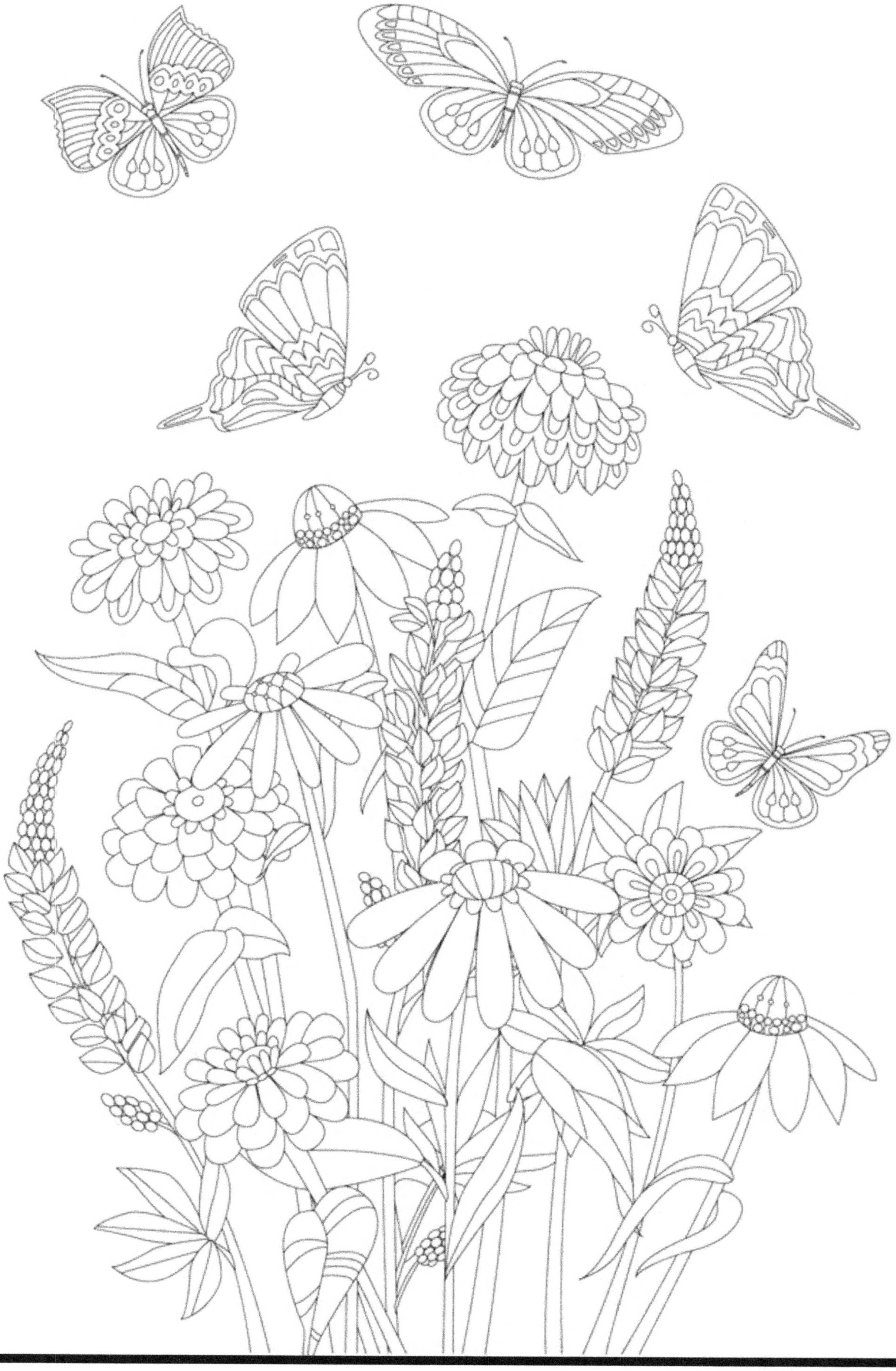

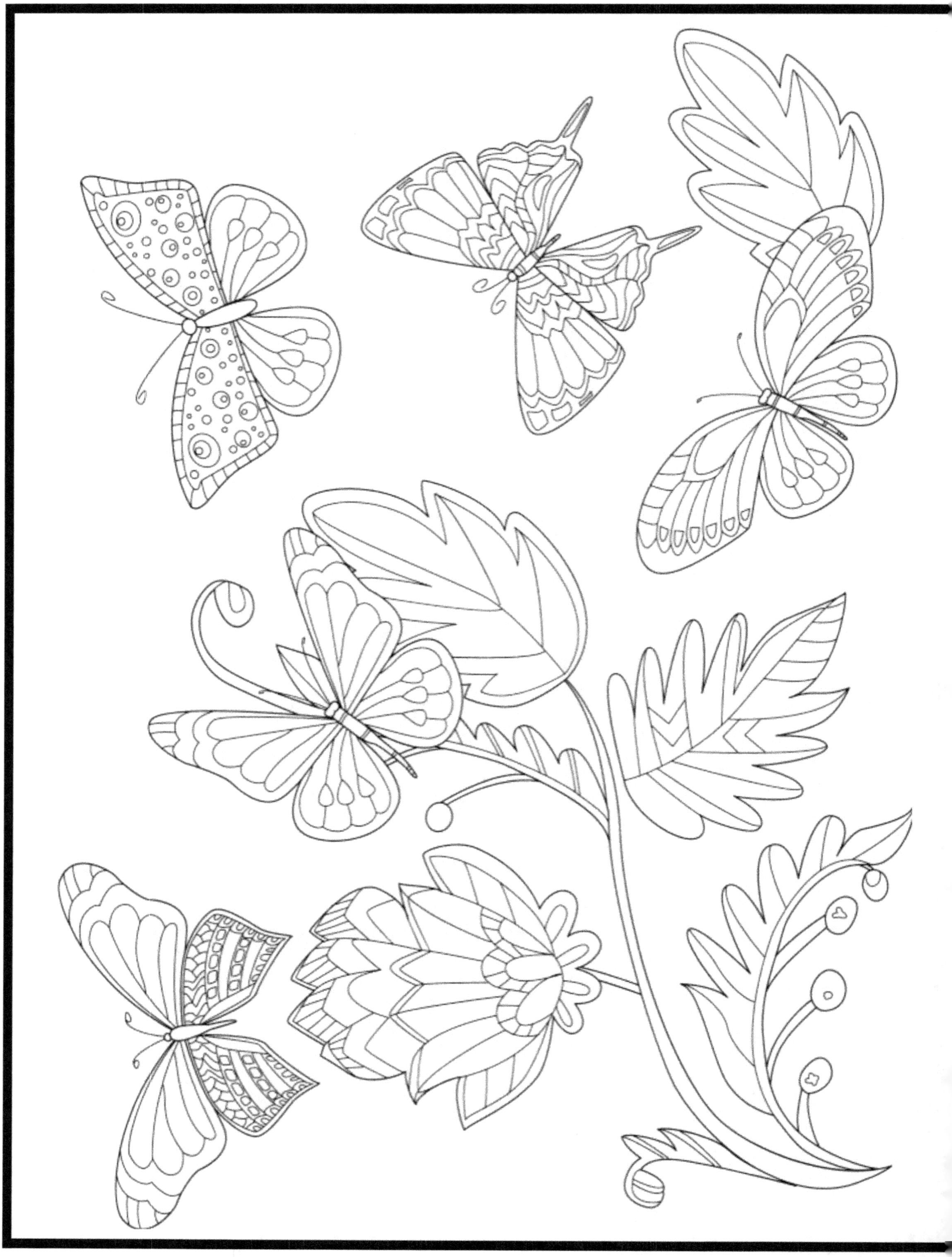

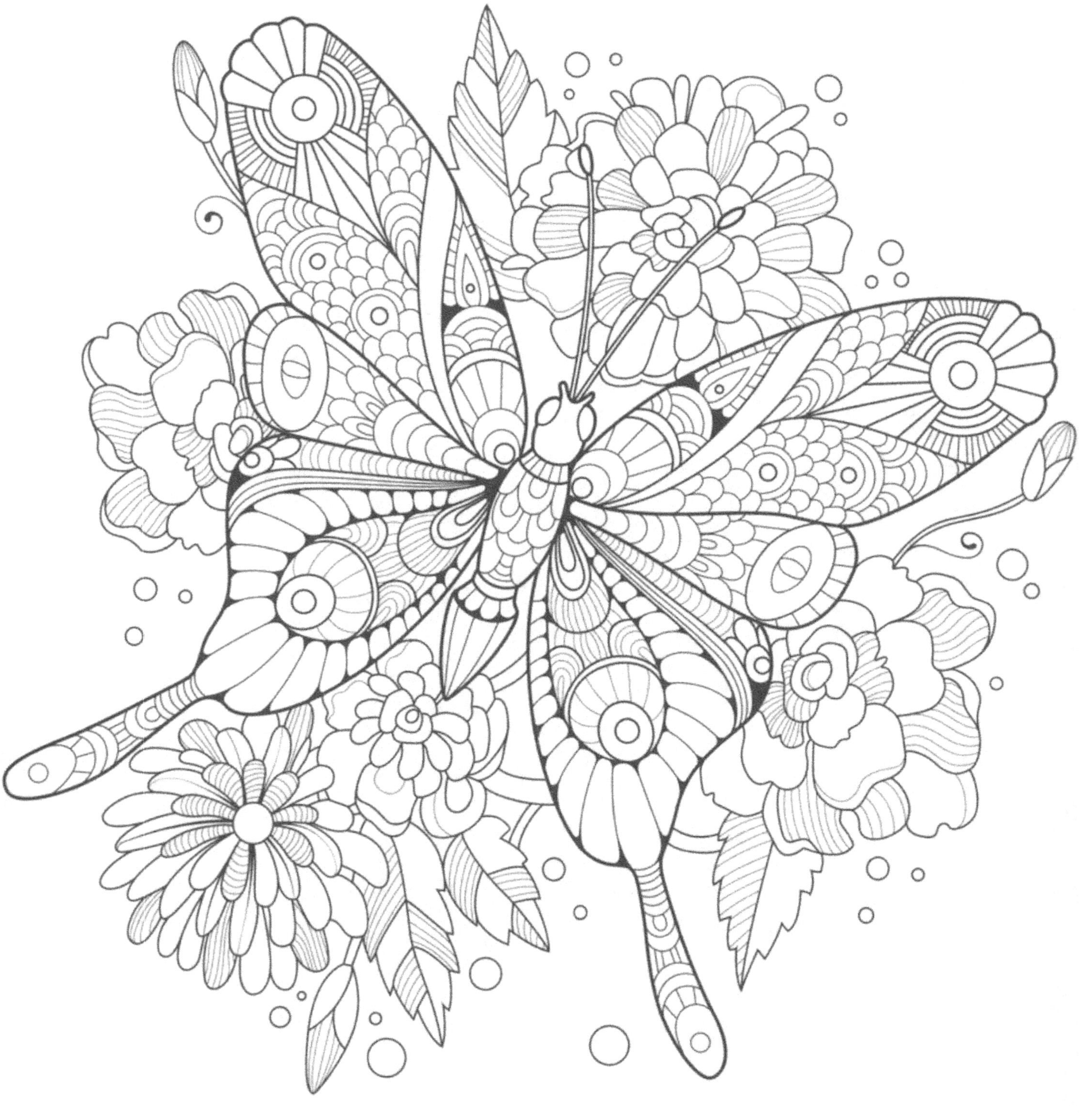

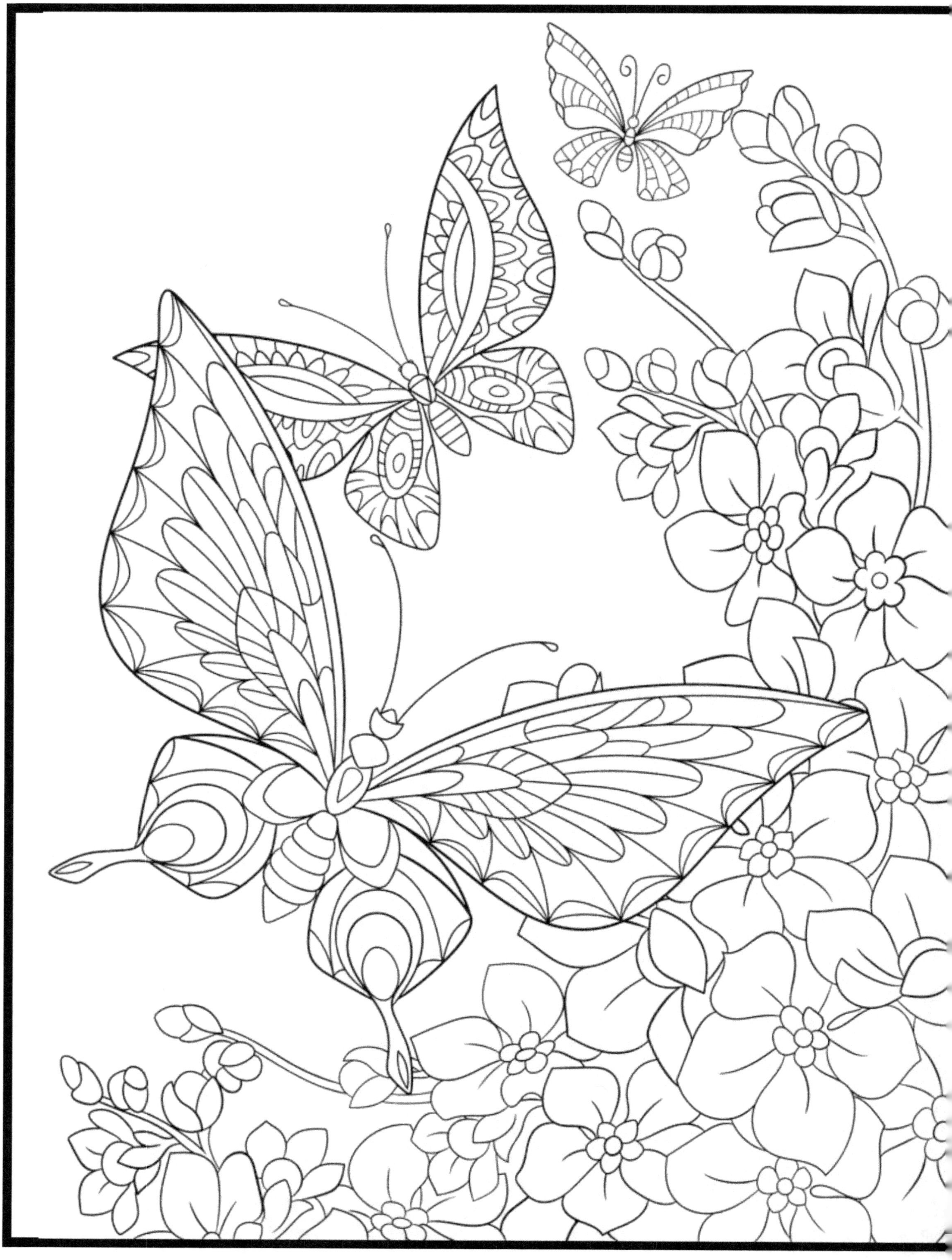

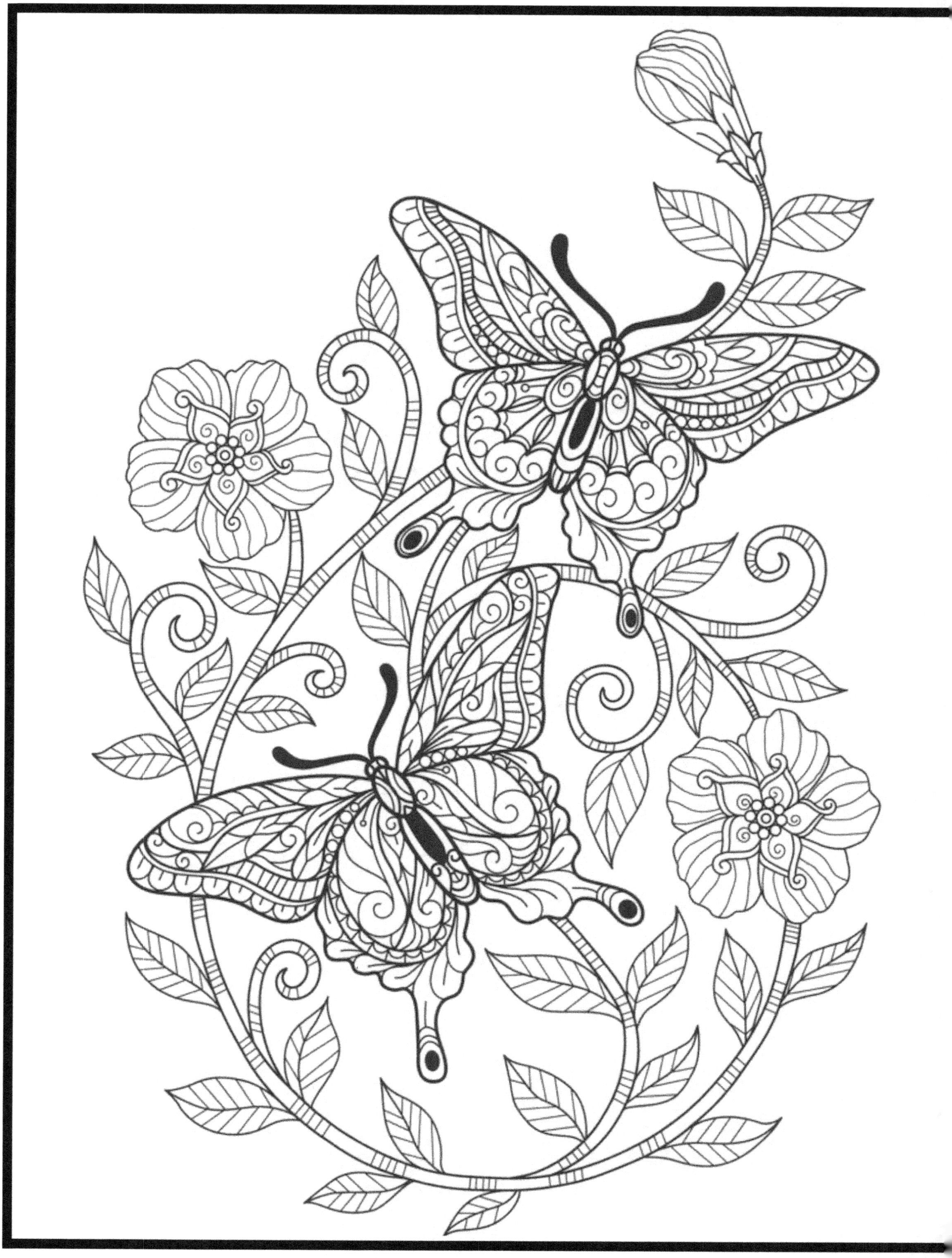

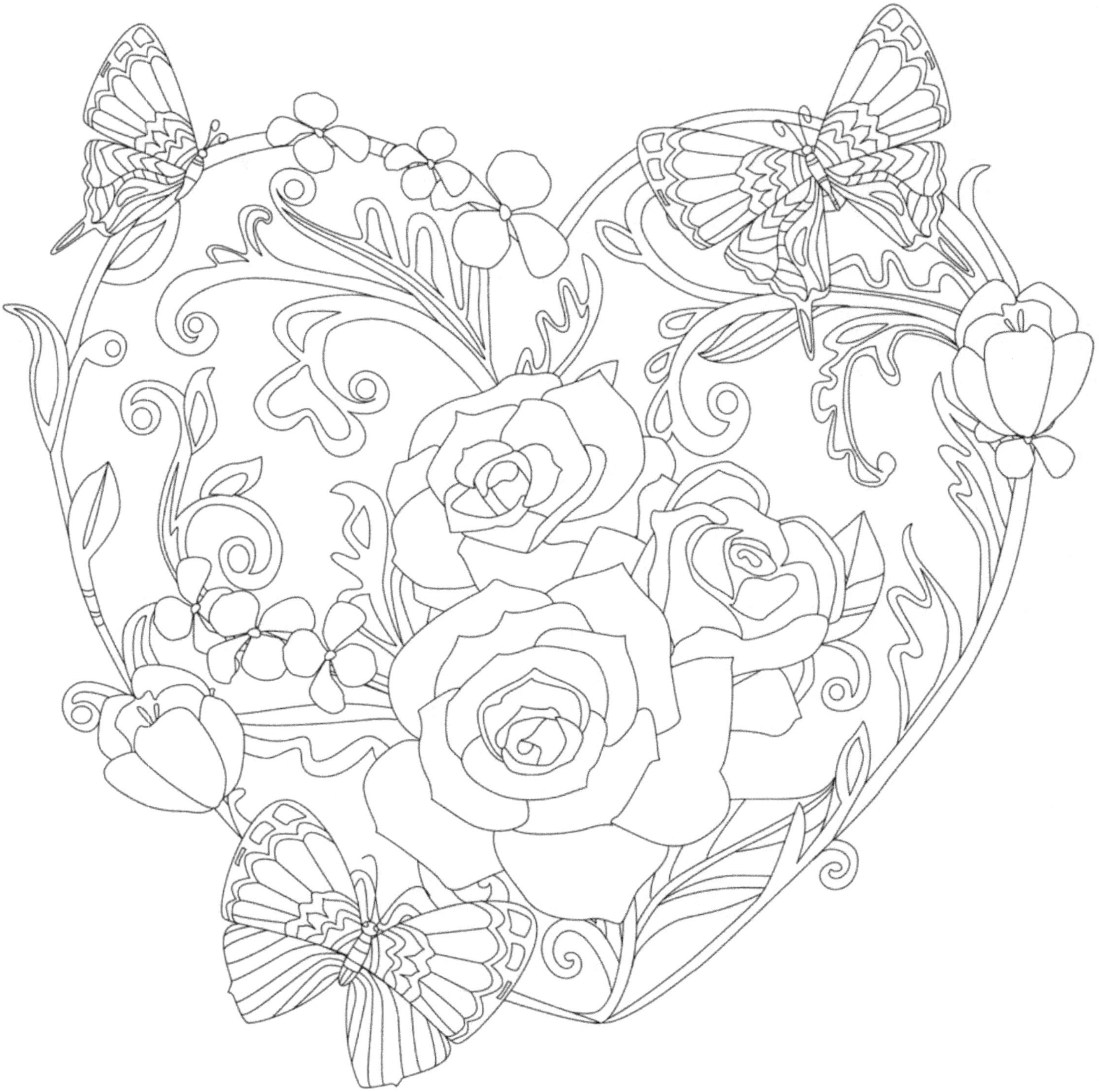

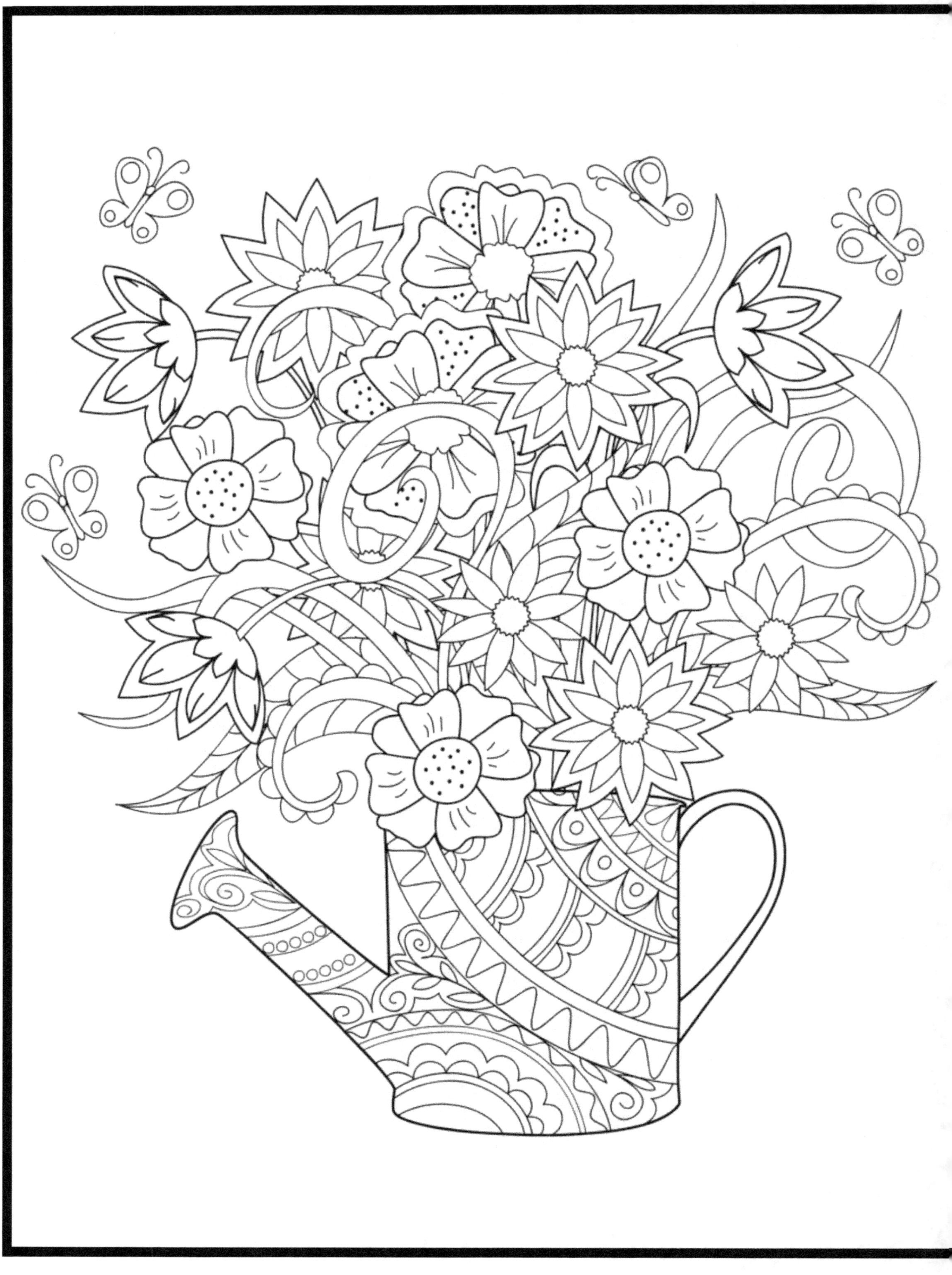

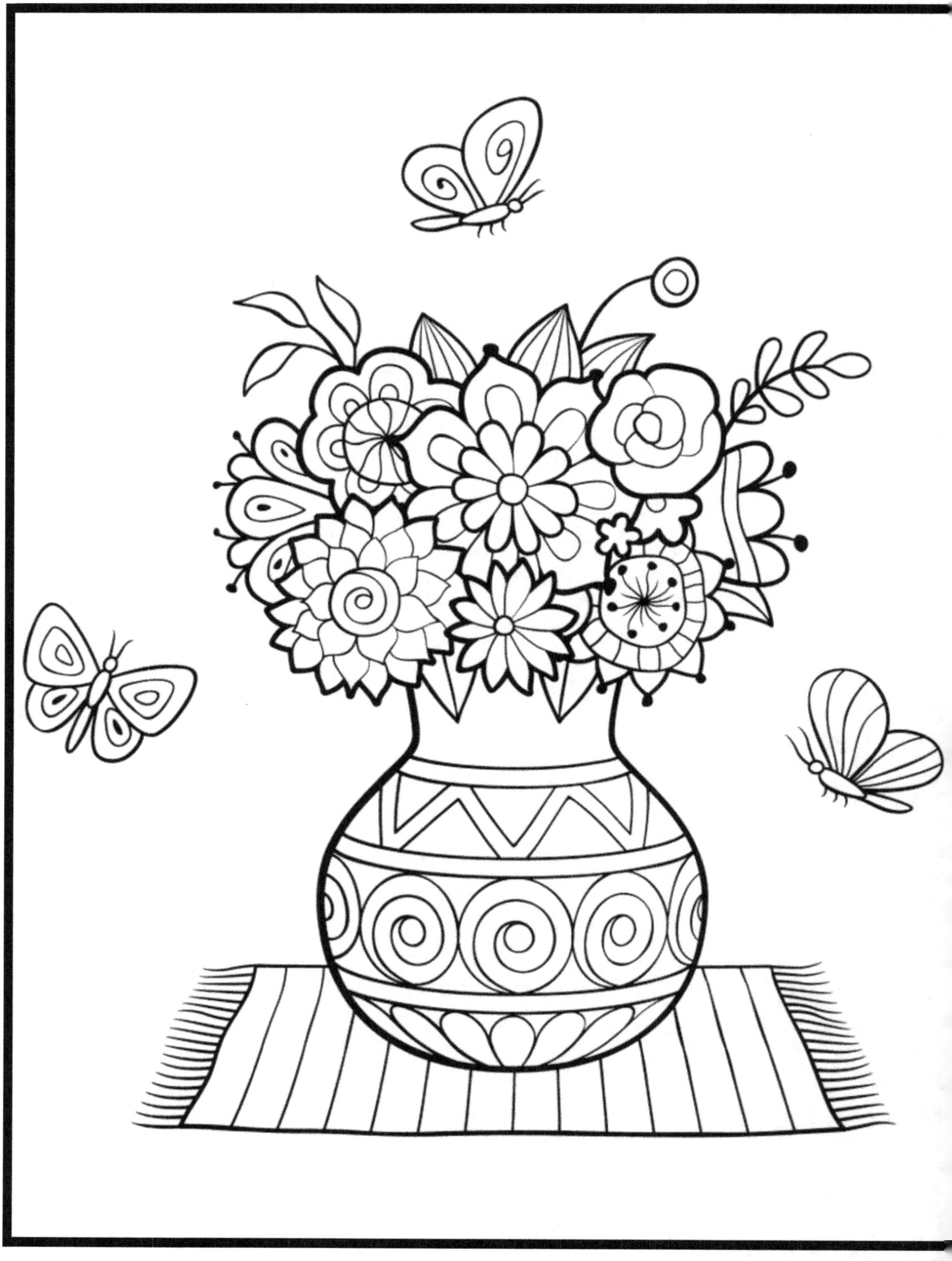

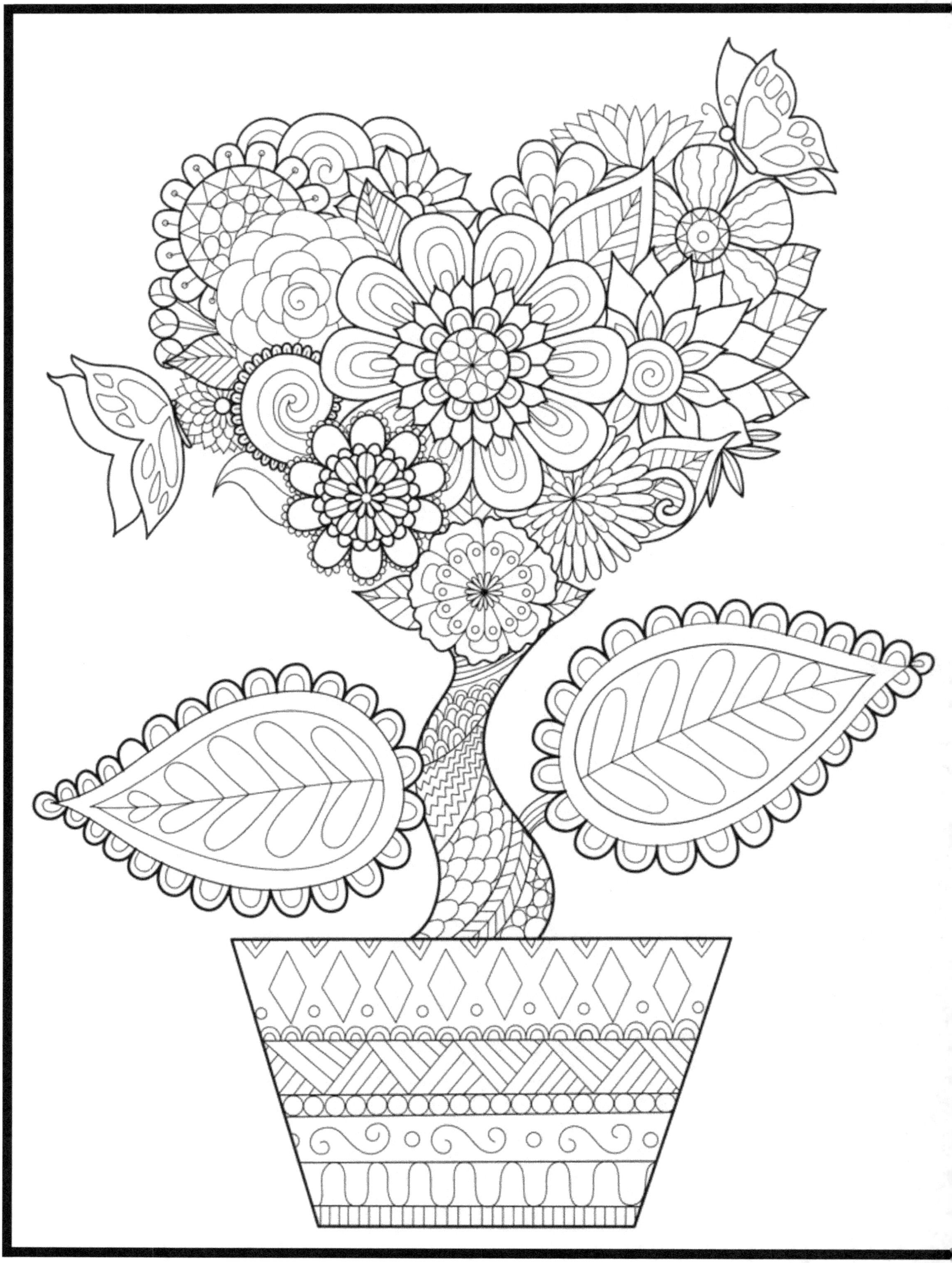

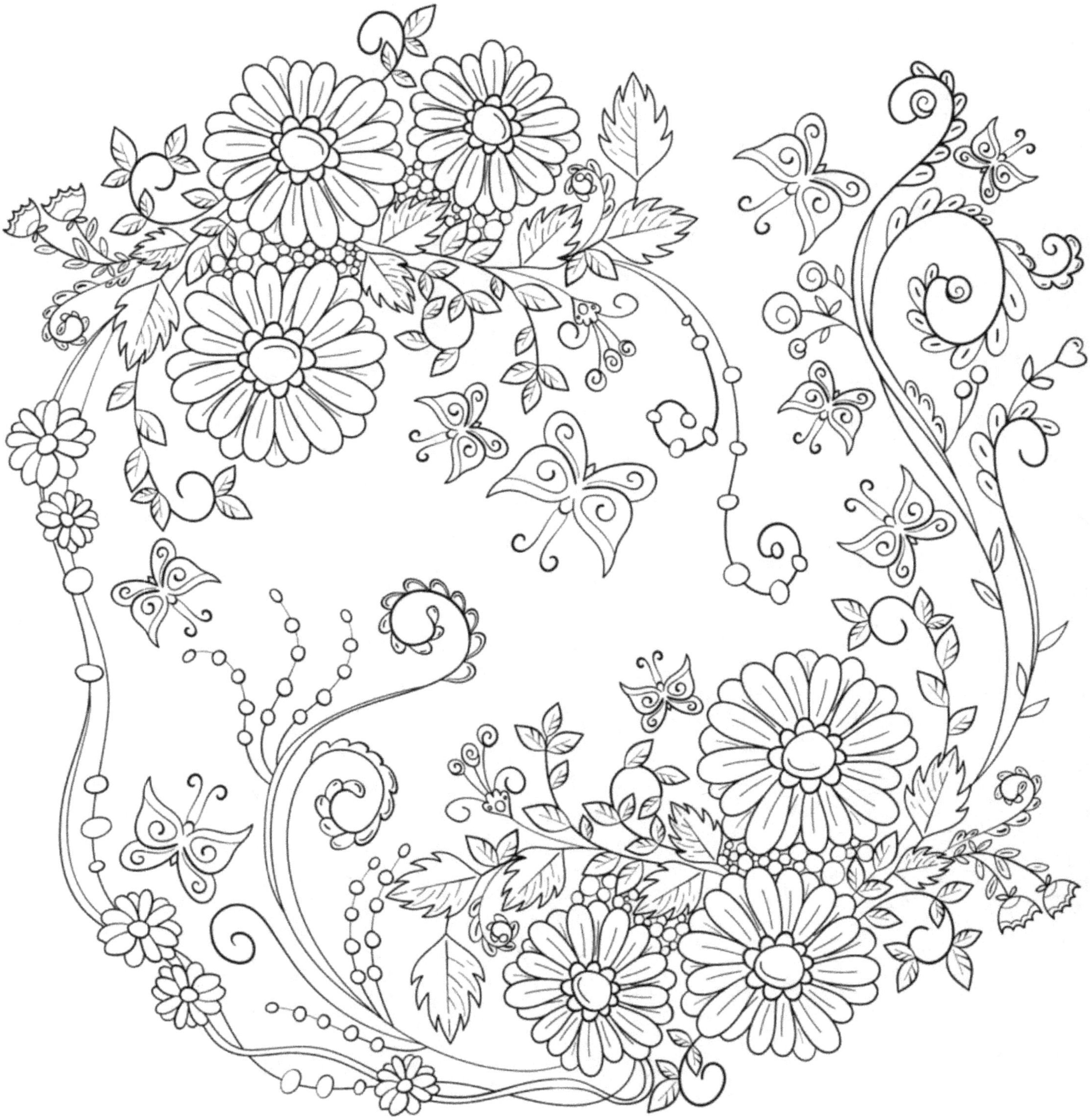

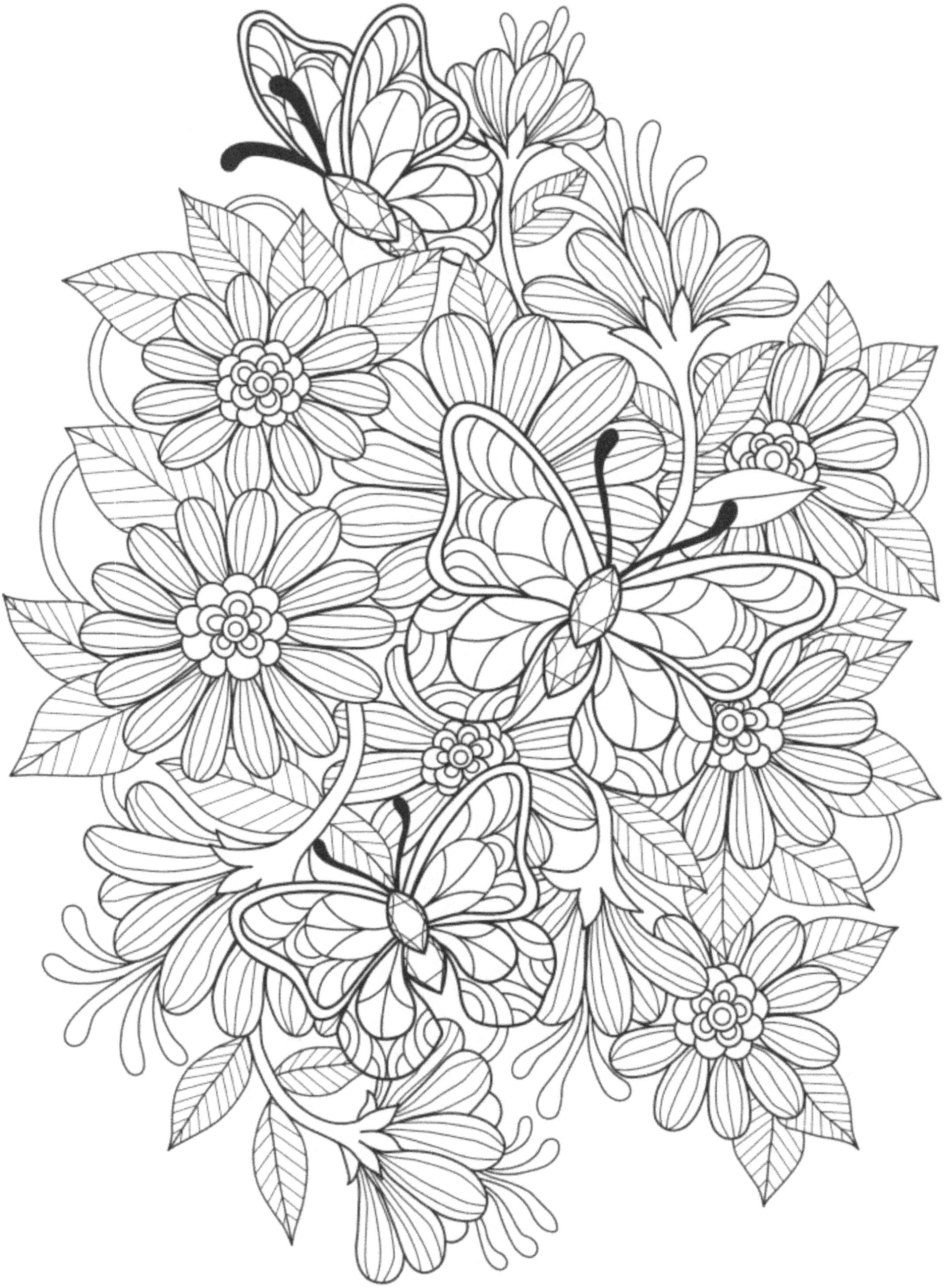

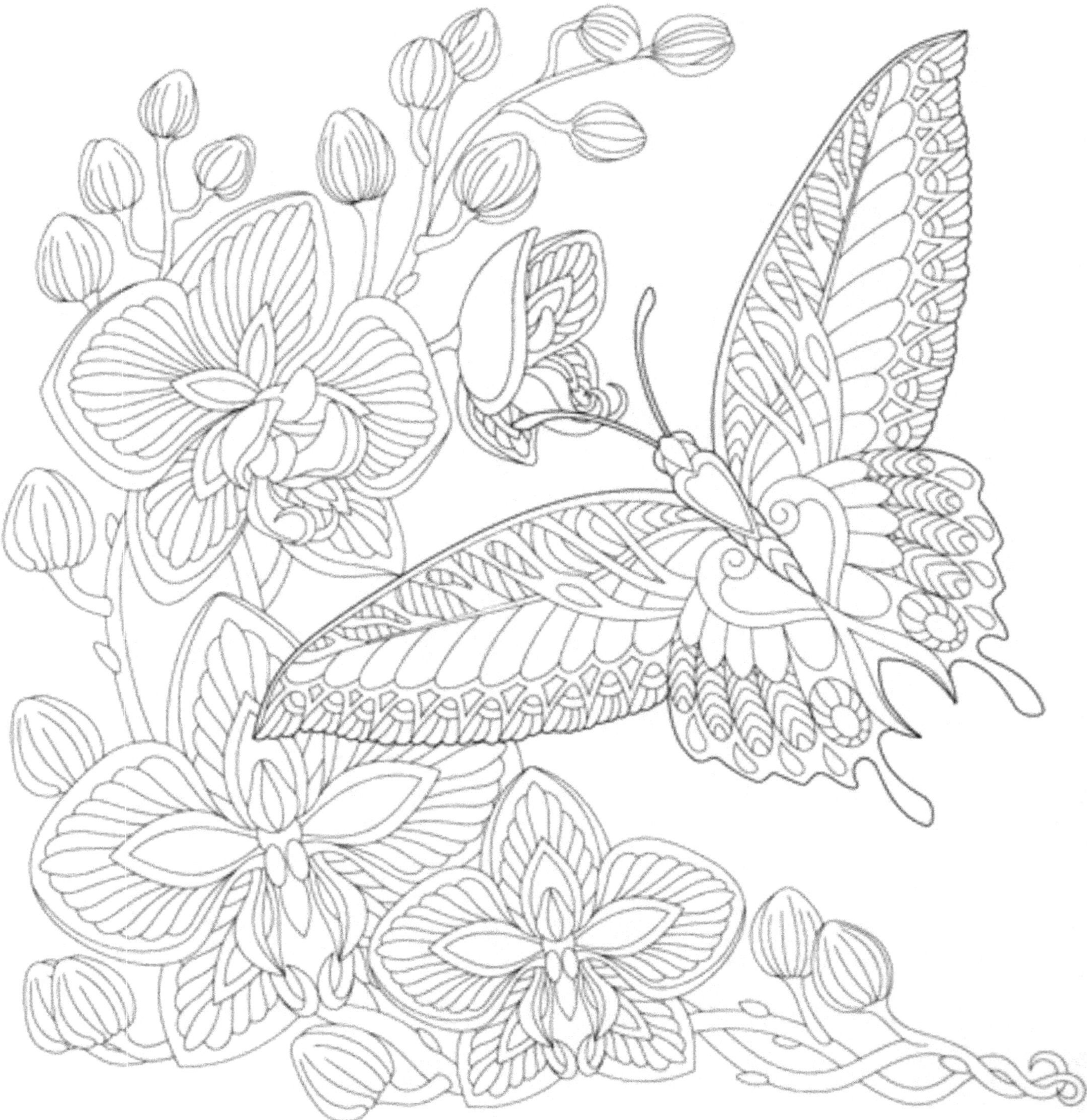

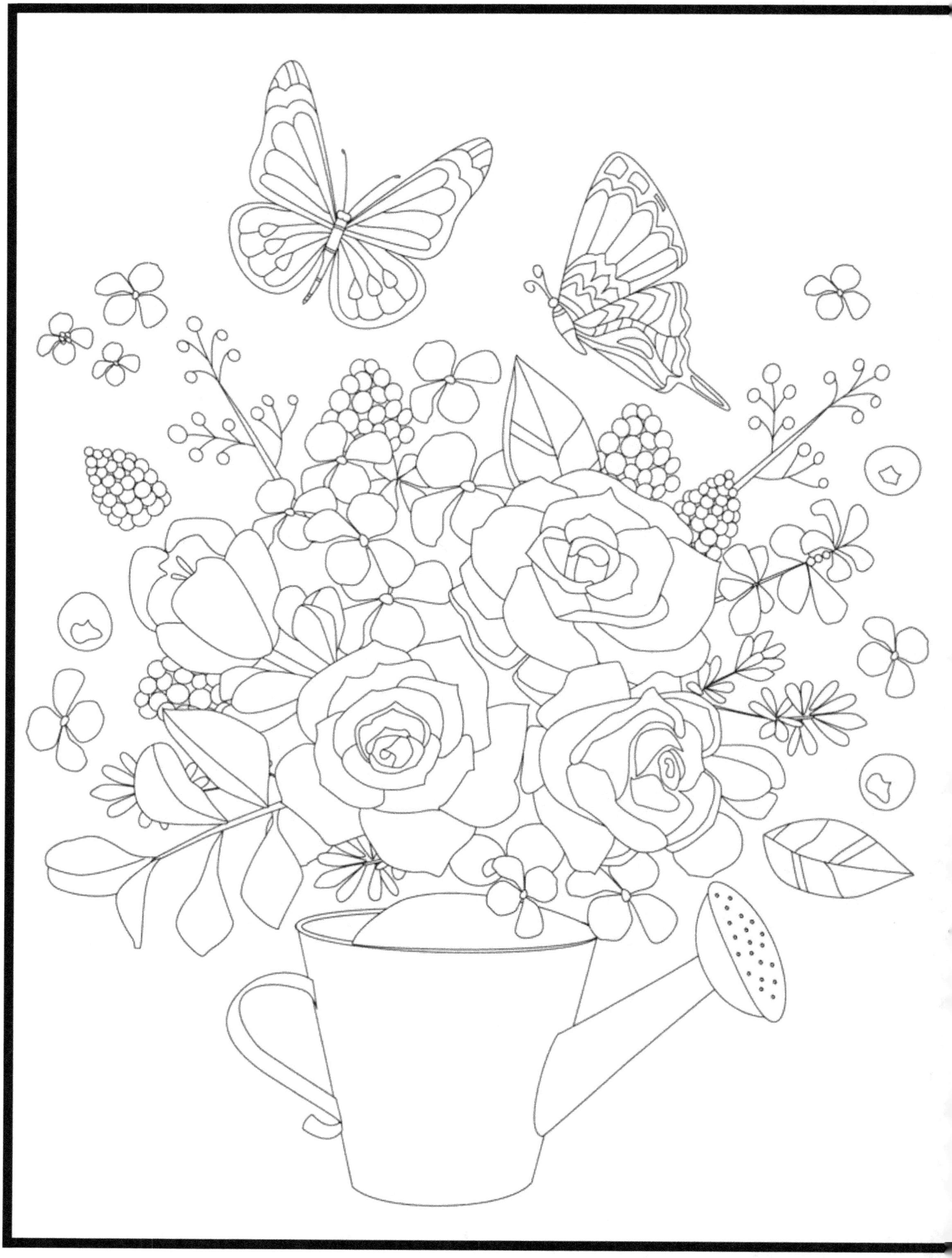

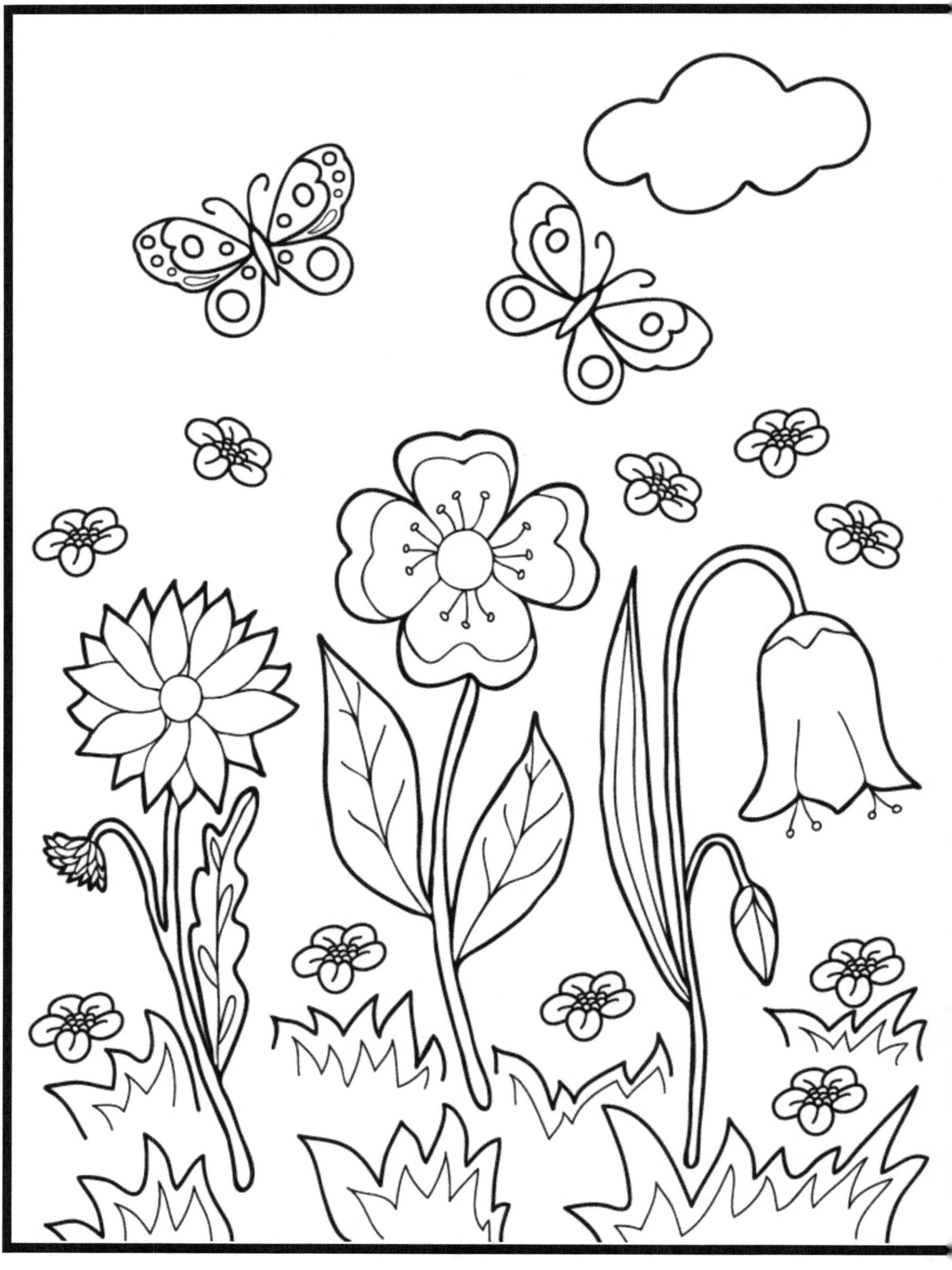

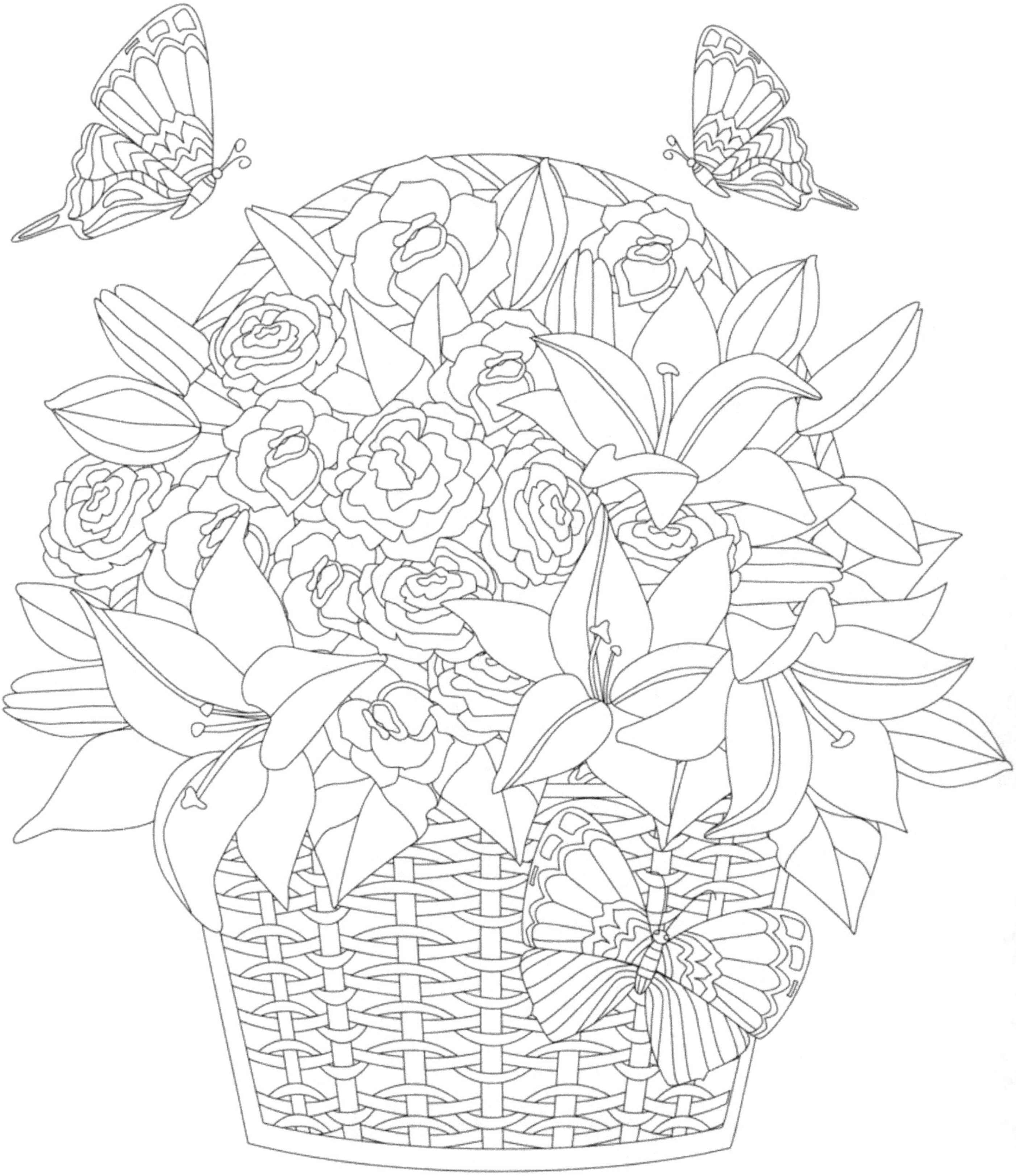

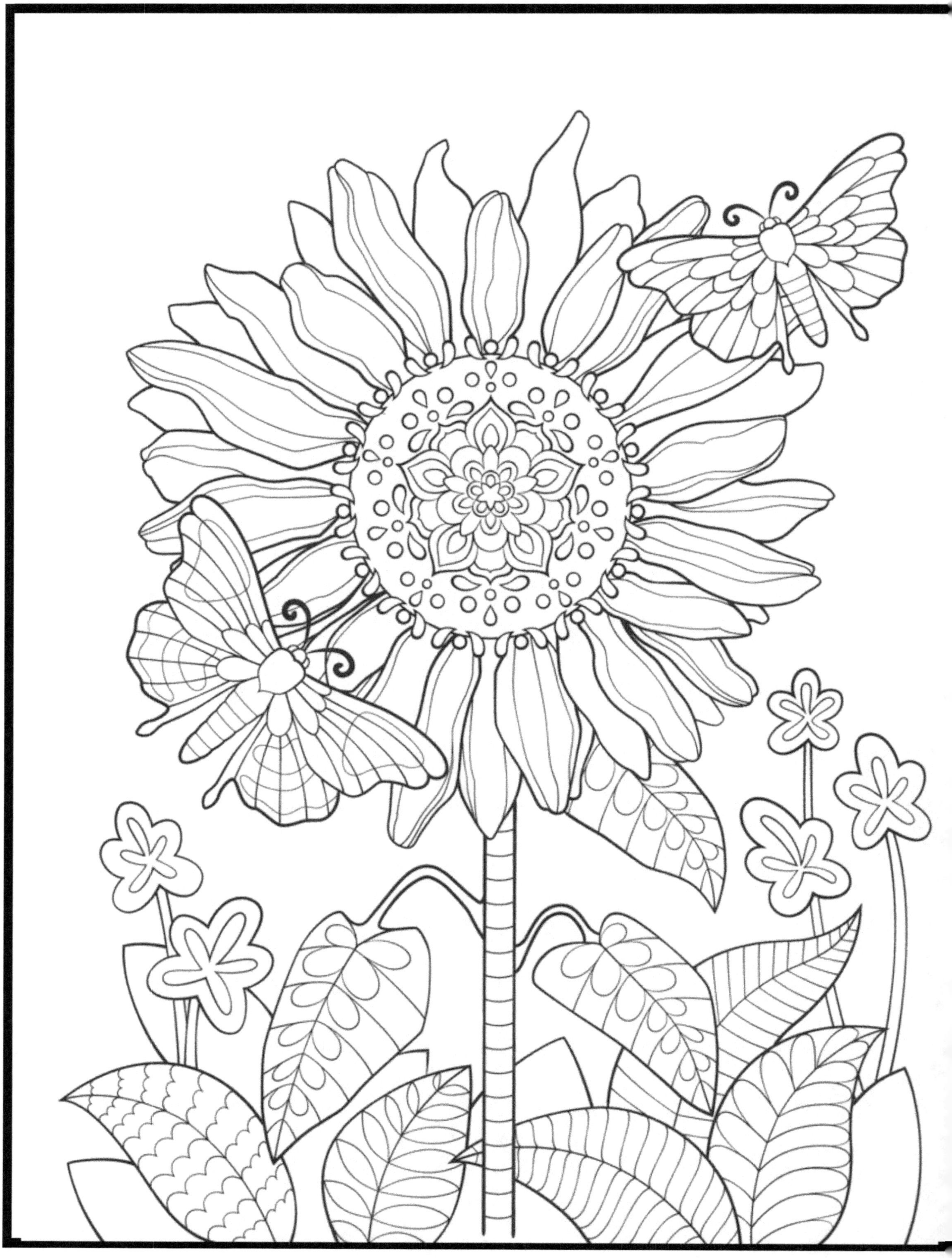

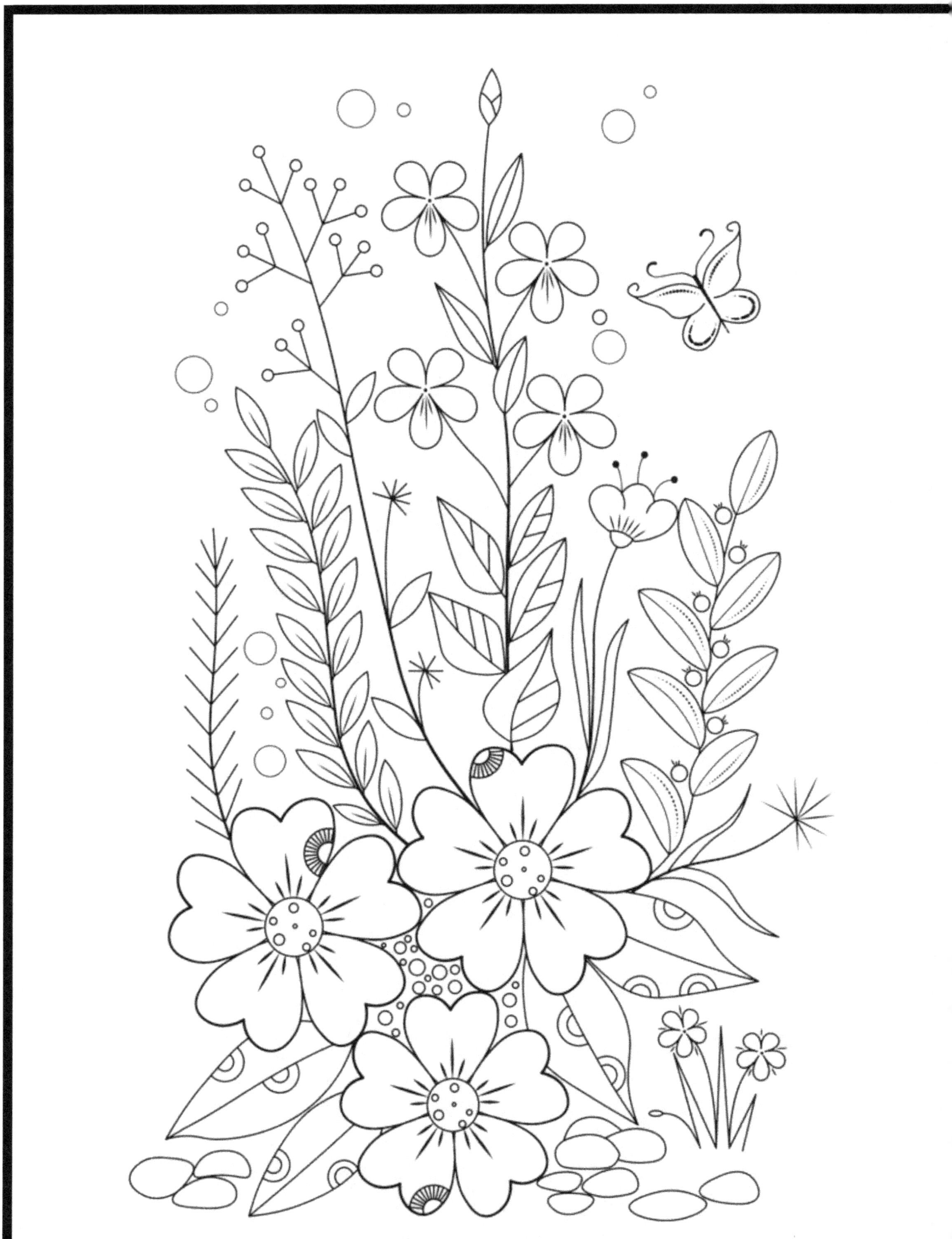

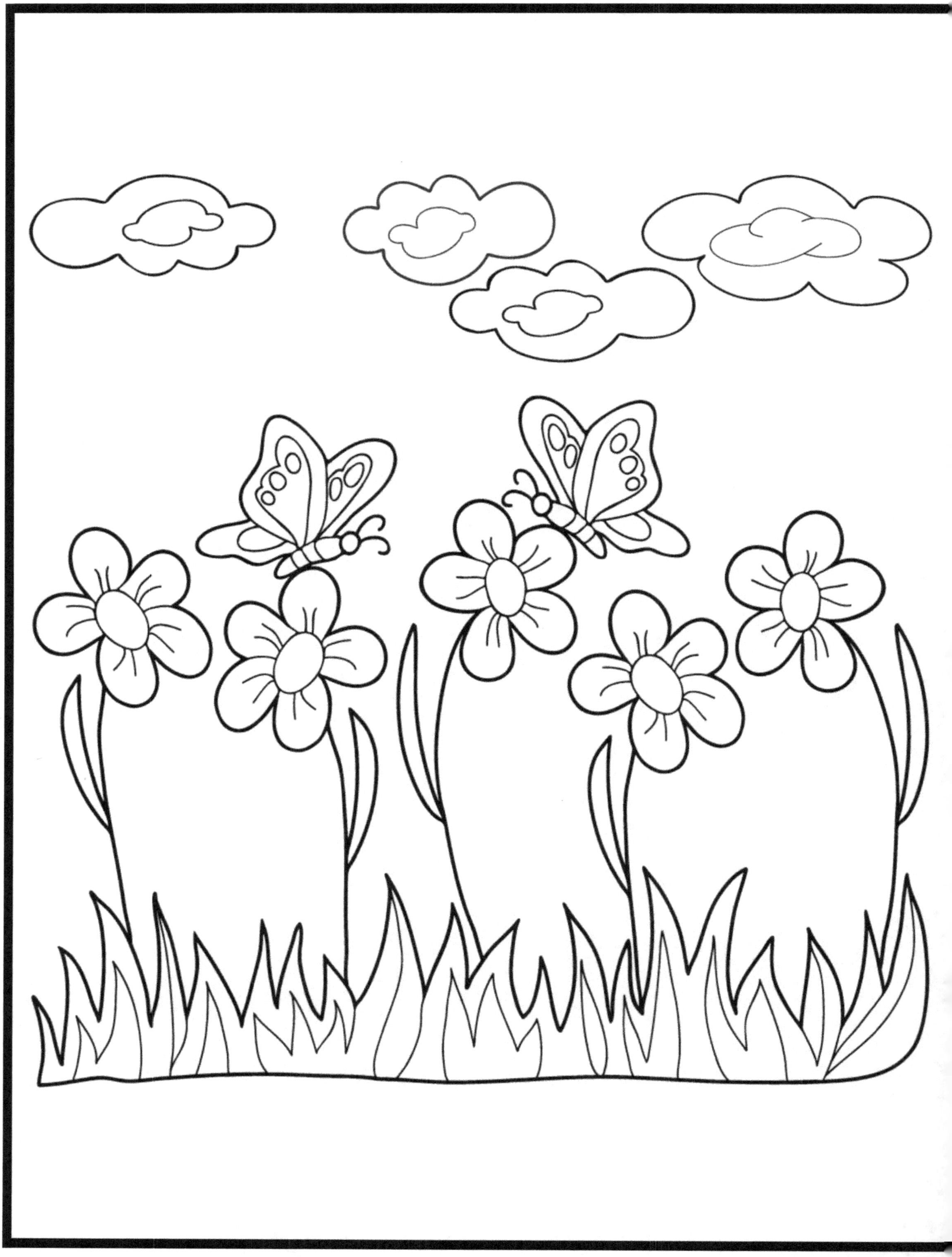

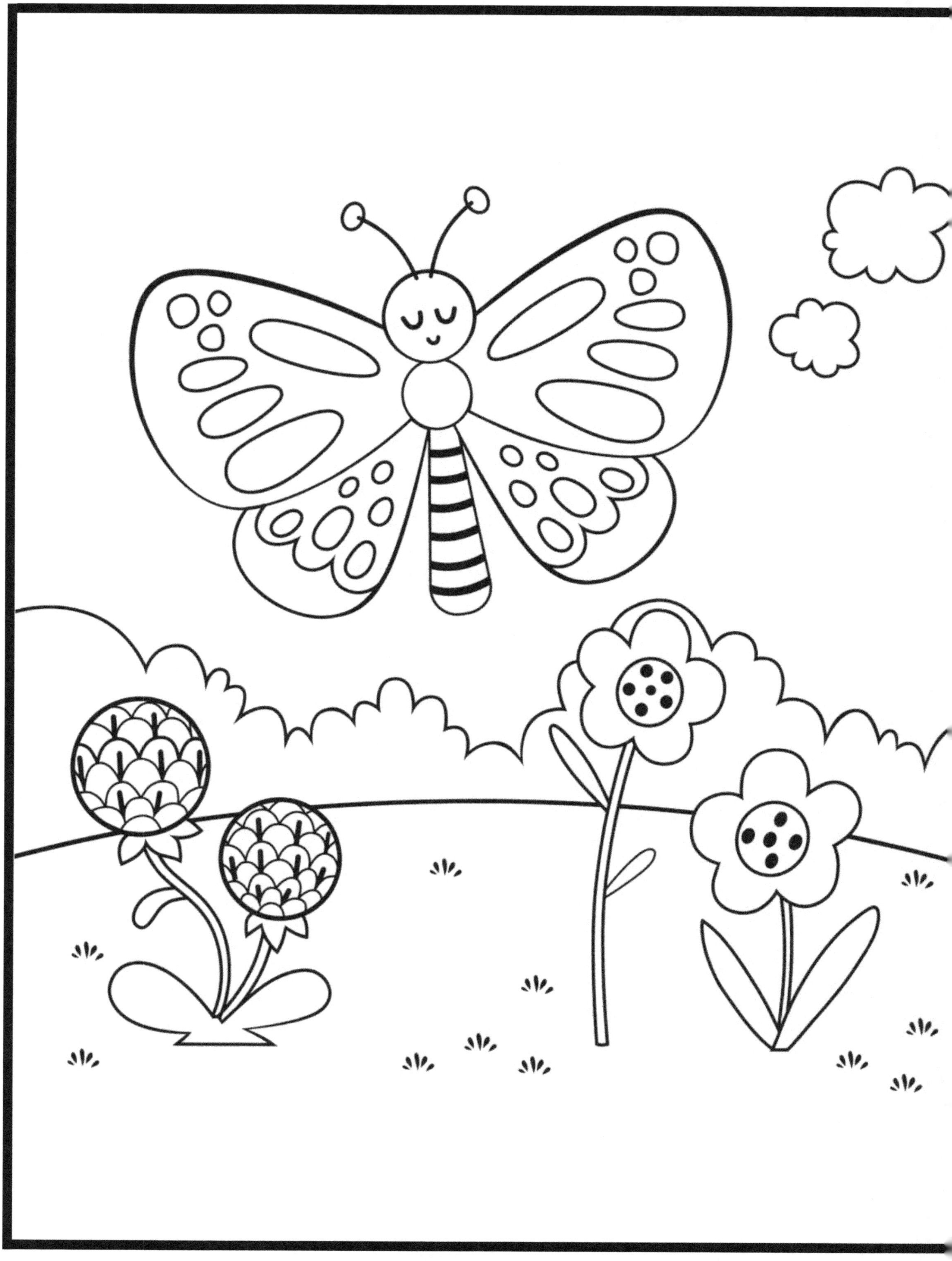

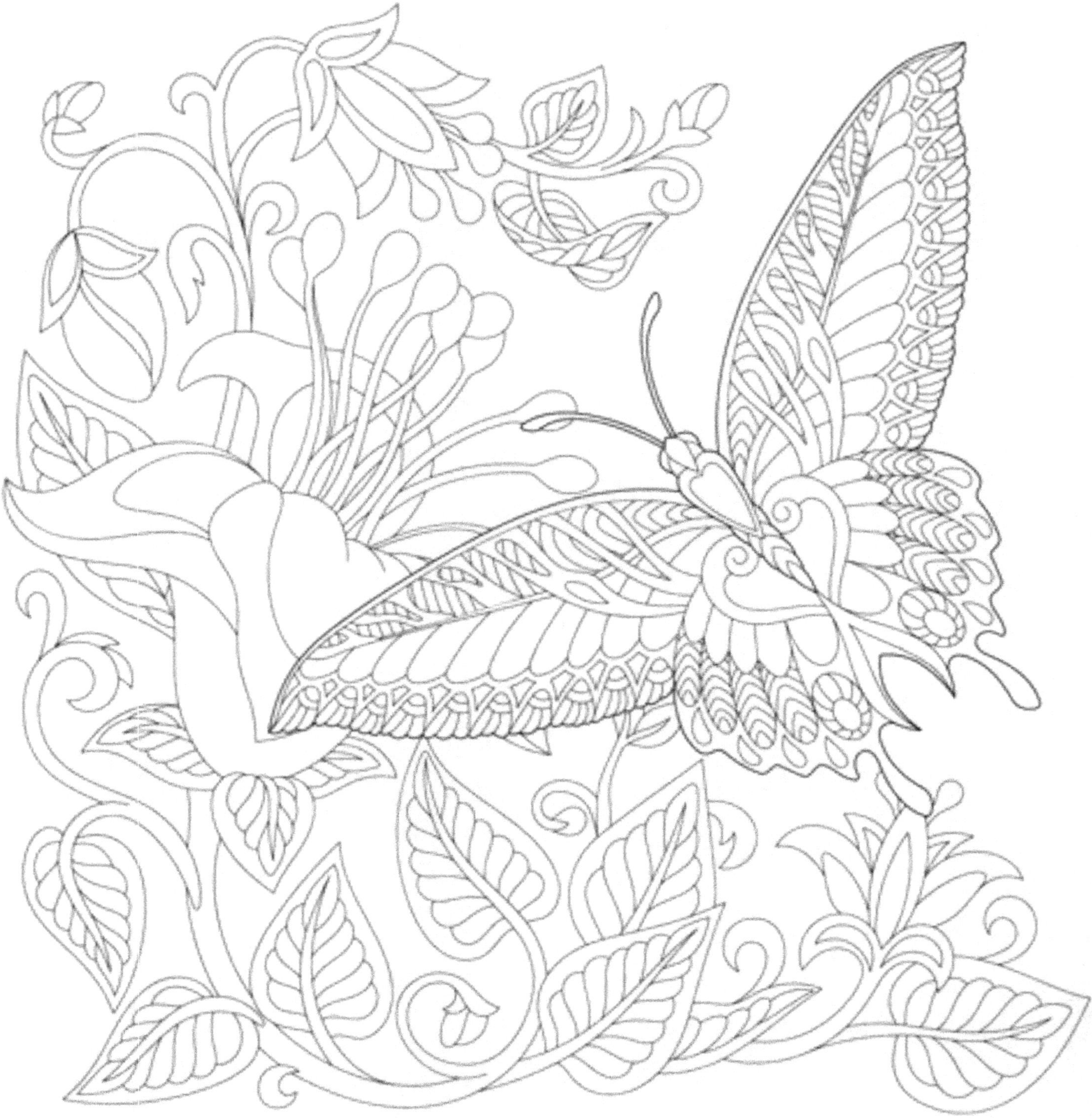

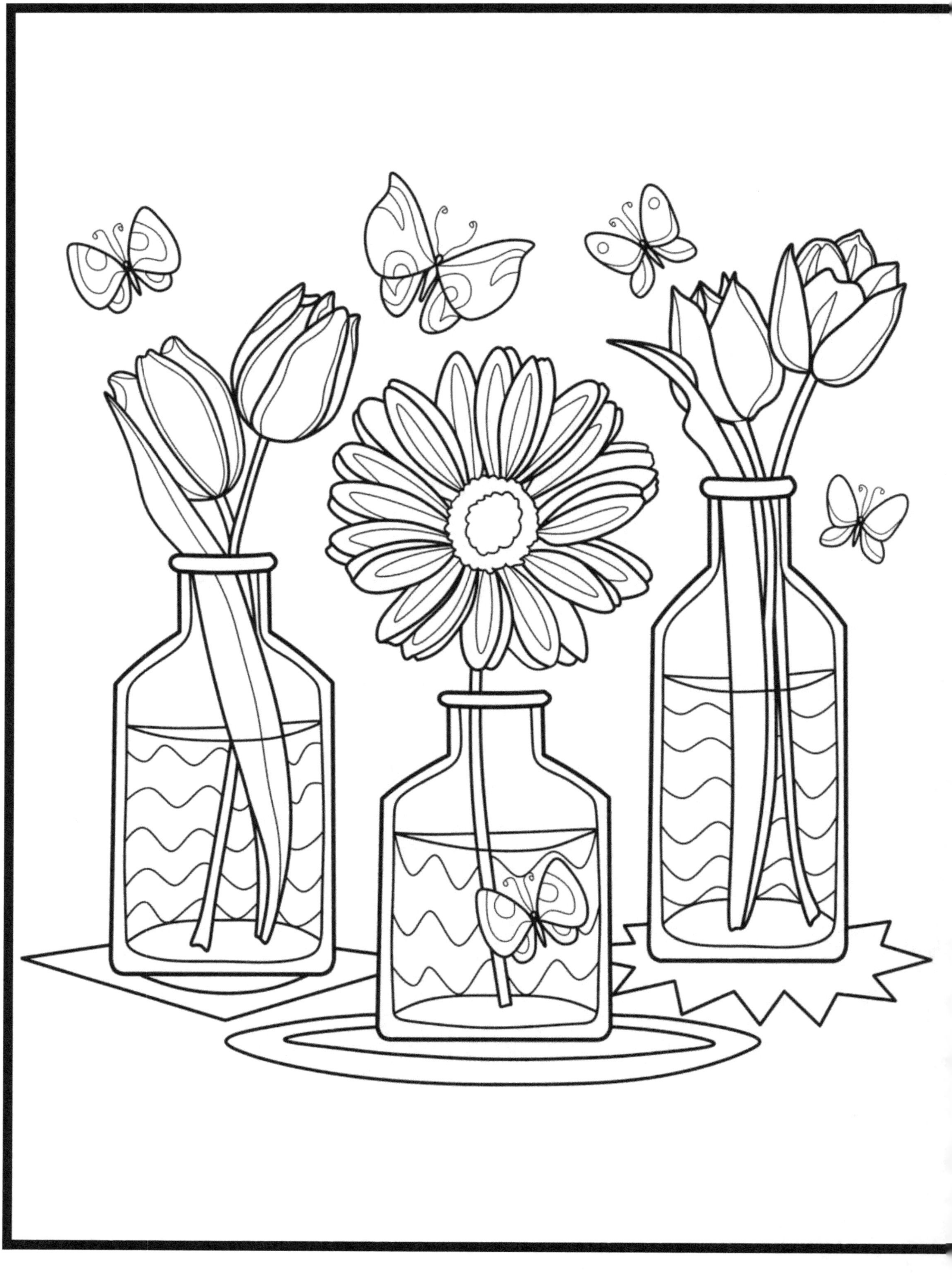

www.ingramcontent.com/pod-product-compliance
Lightning Source LLC
Chambersburg PA
CBHW082215290526
45794CB00009B/3555